POETICAL WORKS 1999–2015

Keston Sutherland

POETICAL WORKS
1999–2015

ENITHARMON PRESS

First published in 2015
by Enitharmon Press
10 Bury Place
London WC1A 2JL

www.enitharmon.co.uk

Distributed in the UK by
Central Books
99 Wallis Road
London E9 5LN

Distributed in the USA and Canada
by Independent Publishers Group
814 North Franklin Street
Chicago, IL 60610
USA
www.ipgbook.com

ISBN: 978-1-907587-90-0

All of the poems collected here were previously published in books and
pamphlets by Barque Press, except *The Odes to TL61P* (Enitharmon Press);
The Stats on Inifinity (Crater Press): grateful thanks to Richard Parker;
'Jenkins, Moore and Bird' which is published here for the first time.

Enitharmon Press gratefully acknowledges the financial support of
Arts Council England, through Grants for the Arts.

Individuals contribute to sustain the Press through the
Enitharmon Friends Scheme. We are deeply grateful to all Friends,
particularly our Patrons: Colin Beer, Sean O'Connor and those
who wished to remain anonymous.

British Library Cataloguing-in-Publication Data.
A catalogue record for this book is available
from the British Library.

Designed in Albertina by Libanus Press
and printed in the UK by
Gomer Press

CONTENTS

Poems collected as [Bar Zero] (2000)

2. THE RICTUS FLAG (2003)

3. NEUTRALITY (2004)

ANTIFREEZE
2002

TEN PAST NINE

In my speech shines a radiant energy,
I can destroy hype, the wind flashes with its end,
fury and barriers become smashed
                out, the music chars hype
broke out from me. I sing and the serrated horizon
tilts, dirt splashes become zero each. We are
okay. I am not even a fucking person any more.
                Without the bloom
of flowers set to crash, and without day after day,
antique throats would char. I am not even
despite fire victimized but am okay. The

grainy void over my speech flares and yellows,
day after day remains, ashen, vital. The things I
do say distort hype, which may become over,
                destroyed that
is to say our worst speech. A face at
my window faces that. Without extrapolation
on me what could become smashed,
                you cut
deep into her tongue with broken glass,
with your fist you strike out. I am ready
today, I can reduce the significance of love.

THE LITTLE MATCH GIRL

Shows you up higher the imperiled second
outbreak in misery how we each can destroy
that they said, by perilous star
flipped out across an outbracketed sky,
                    by the adamant wayside,
where in tolerated adroit opposition
they said we stand or fall, the wall can become
transparent like gauze,
stops there and readies herself for conflict
                    resolution it says
you picked that formalized modes of
arbitration, formalized modes of erotic happiness,
the star bangs you think highly
across or sideways can an adduced fire thread
                    they ask you
to envyless sedition, as the preferable
sun budges out, can it thread you to distort out
you're breaking up try no try okay
thread you to the panic of indefectible
                    vanity, as in love the skyslide
impossible you are they
say, lights were shining from all
the windows and the dark
brown leaves in the hearth
                    catarrhal screw up and flash.

In the brief glow, imaginative corruption to near
zero visibility of the proletariat
wednesday I came to my senses they said no
to her, contributing by impractical echo
            to rapid and shallow
breath urgent dyspnoea send the thuds in good
you see an impersonated face
elicit combustion of the origin of mediated
expression boy took her right slipper
            profuse hectic sweats,
nothing to eat in the house but consolidated relish,
she wanted to keep herself warm, they said
and very far from inert the stricken
fence hinted at convenient distress and downfall
            raked through blood
saw teeth there, I saw a complete hand made
me wait and scared, trash cozens
dingo budgie flares up fuck you shut up it,
friends enter the room
            used was milk of sulphur
they said lights were shining from all
the windows, the dark then became reduced,
for them thought of highly,
once this fastened see the imperiled star,
            diremption of industrial and political

conflict. See the shadow of remorse,
preened, tremulous and frigid
tiny feet are stretching there, a match beside
them tinkles baghdady, the patient
                    feels this glow of heat run
away through both sides of chest,
the affinity in 1914 of hydrogen and precipitated
sulphur, they were so big they
from my feet, destroyed by cartwheels,
                    can this be the day
light crapped over a grille town say no
they said they were communicated barricaded
faces they town moved into
long streaks of fire across an incorruptible sky
                    this violence has
declined, and has been replaced by formalized
modes of arbitration, you are
among them, the modes reach out for you
in unutterable love they reach out for
                    you please take them
scratches a divisible face, they are said
here, from the apices of both lungs
brilliantly consumed and without this vanity of
any kind smashes that, may she out
                    spoken for now, just say yes.

SLITS IN THREES ODE

You mitigate the fever of the scrub, truck, bulletin
faraway idiot, you as teeth comb
gashes through preserves, make finalized light

stroke of cracked, of feed puerile
damage to you no end overmuch visible carry
out days achieve fact to fact be there,

be polemical, issue the wind decree,
floats through eternal stop you are bind
are crash of the exchange, feasible tang and shut

gray out, jump about the room
picking an exact slot forever go in treacly
has you by a liberated throat.

2

Only you mess up the oil scare, lonely
tags a face envisages and default beet, tonic
universe fiasco, the wind cut

feasibly into strips do an outlook
do always committed to blank and amorous
where the gray shone, are help

them not to die fish
parcels littered bounce up a star queasy
squashed and ground in decide you

could prepare a change round
mouthful of amateur maggot honey for
now okay scrap you, rubrics at dawn.

3

As an abated scruple whose perhaps you
saw it derange a valid rainbow,
whose descry quickly be a love format take

you saw them face explode it
rained night and to morning jump over
the sky that flip crease

ever since the day collides whose finished
type of visibility airs are
screw the wind down, do exact cancel out,

bandage the hurt water, thereupon
cannot bitch too prosperously
make you reluctant wipe that grin off.

4

Stretch only to that famish divert
everything it is you must possibly accept,
bollocks to the flame strawberry

rots out panic finesses the Chávez article
bus depot, clippers,
what a face either way be a squeeze in

into the chivalrous rigmarole of validity,
into the pristine offshoot you
is that the time, do cryptonormative

flinches you bargained for, do
the stars remain alert and well travestied
ratio of dysgenic oyster to Islam.

5

What the trick is to produce a scintillant,
beneath cloud cover allegorizing mission time,
onto whose knees or in fleshy

spate of you be that rudder in cop boreas,
loosing avert loosing strip
them of pain and agitated counterreckon do

key errors to recall three of which
am not yet blind, pushed too
rapidly for heavy industry two retained

government structures of the colonial era,
three, failed to predict sharp
rise in interest, sink out in a depicts flash.

6

Mutilated hourly false control, verified
chip away verges cast out
verges to remain however free, past

the streetlight courses upon arcades runs
alerts the client backdoor shot
like a bolt through were you vivid on

cue drub expiry and incipience, they are clearly
no match for a mute disquiet,
nor for the scar spangled rescind guy pass

sentences on fire, you then borrowed the trowel,
and so throw up an assuaging sea
of ways to make a breathless living.

7

Vanish you life incorrupt, specializes in makes
of which like often or lately,
emending the tree packet, scoops net out

brought to fastidious outrage monkey shit
the shower rips up you hand,
very much want to become impassible

Oh! nicht einmal die Gnade, mit dir
freight lolls about you loll about
panic in the future rivet, a stream thorny go

into awaiting deals and pass fire,
bits of that vacate are solemn their nozzle out
shines burnish it, gag you are live act.

A LOVE SONG

As never the day collapses throw
        instead your face down,
fashion a blind the brevity of
        you may diminish, the USAF drops

away and far too much I
        ravenously vex nothing except you,
shook your head and flashes
        drop or a grated star

you had me manic with happiness
        in us dissevered,
from the spit of a longwinded sky
        and elsewhere its summary

flashes also cut a blind
        down and the trimming scapelark
you see drops, you alone
        see, and so do we love together.

A BANG COVERS ME

You were through the rectangular slot down
partway to the side where the echo fit
not envision you. I could do with that. You
                    pay what for
now may attention, were thrown against
people all flashing and melting. Does
that hurt. Does it matter now too, hyped too
                    shut up about
were paralyzed. The division of separate
face it you can fuck me anytime, are
you how late you are, please, stop. Indirect

blast injuries chiefly due to roof destroy,
by crushing and trapping head. Some
place beneath there, through so the dreamy
                    prevents you
cannot see where you are. Shout out your
forget. Does the situated light can,
secondary to the devastating blazes over
                    look in my eyes,
patch up the broken glass, at ease they
do not ask who seizes them. You can
want to do it here. Make up your mind.

LOSS OF LIFE

It's loss of life not to be yours cringes the ripped tin,
     inert it remonstrates feel battered, become long
          since passed echoes the sandwich-paste too
and flight to the repaired wish cancer settling
     up striking the bill, washing the out-screened
          promises she'll not make lightly arranged
to say that: assume you drive a total of thirty-six
     miles to and from work each day
          and that it takes an hour to do so your

hourly risk of dying in a traffic takes the bongo
     flips fistfuls of warped coins, crash while
          driving say that each year you do that two
hundred ways to be like some ice vented my
     street scrounges a face back, some feet,
          teeth made of plastic, arrogant loss of life
expectancy flutters through a head spilled open
     to suggest you cannot, desperate for consummate
          love alone, match that total risk.

SEX CRATER

Lick the gag and lascivious flame fades,
I am shut it goes. Fastened to, snapped
shut by and stuck on her. She makes
up my life pitted for one instinct, see how
does this continuously, rubber shreds
and scandalizes the chewed glass the car
head out through the windscreen.
Her face goes on my leg. Broken
ice scattered in molten chrome glows,
    falsified the compact
    body you bargain
    away chip-eyed and wasted,
    so drunk the
street in an invisible ice-storm and
men and women entranced to a death-fad
go about nothing unheard. Delete the
exit every step of the routine reinscribes,
make a fresh end, link the shadow
vomited from the eye to an erotic highlight
went shut. Moth versus spaghetti: it
says here shut the thing open to greased
suggestions to the same contrary,
    as trusted the light shies,
    waving across
    her face and my single
    is a hit. But forever.

A COUNTDOWN TO REPEAT

Wait. The choice is disbelieved like the palliative
ice glued into my throat and when acid
say gossip confronts them, tearing apart the real divide
incompletely was a stuck on you
are yourself what faces. Wait. I am behind my back,
reshift of crap outward inexact vague, too
sideways to clutch at to recollect when to you
fabulously hate looked made up. Now improbable
light shines, heat itself melts,
in the drafted amnesia do a withstood picnic wait in
fleshy tones and relaxed in time and
                    and cold glare blindingly over
                    that windscreen flips, distorted
way out like mutual trust. The leaves are all
paranoid, crunchy and when you pick lapses
gone to hate nothing can fix. What among this
strip of things to break draped in my
face is broken at all. Wait. This is a question, can
it be where disconsolate and breaking
faces all are, pitted within the wait thread to finish
you as days can. It was the contract in Bahrain
that Harken won through Bush, who then
admitted its directors to U.S. foreign policy
                    meetings of minds
                    deranged as an abacus made out
of ice balls and electrical wire, please can
I recover myself hurt whit-boy. The leaves are
rehanged, unconturbated maybe dianoid all
the stars pop. You're so jammy. Wait. There
make that thing. I am extraordinarily
happy alive. I went out and found new people

excited beyond went out, found new
people what they are never that. In the end,
when finally the tangs are slick you
            see finished lights on and
            people you love in a smashed queue.

DO YOU BLOSSOM

As the chosen form of panic car
crash to my rear frozen
out by words too beautiful to spot
are you alone, take off your
chance to wheel through
clouds in unvanishing havoc up
the street in the love
        people too no
        end alone
chancing apart them
and far lived you fetch for
the last time another
night positioned over the lilac
and nothing and bake
you shift out of the wrong window
pellet to a drop end
        life each
        strapping day but
and the ice is gluey so
and the volcano rain is gateaux
far to the way differently
seceded can you taste how
aftertastes vanish outside the rain
in fact chooses to hit rock
bottom on the list of
        uses the break as
        mere toyish

shift to go being on with
and the people to the left
hand side of their own faces bleed
helpfully and ponderous
ash like a whisper steers
immediately the correct heat in you
through no hoop, I love you.

AN ACCIDENTAL ELEGY FOR GATT

Several nights over the apart lounge tags along
caches of foisted dust were people swerving
to each other can you cry still a blank countermand

draped on celery pending are what you cry out
love echoes under the bridge over the motor
way in a straight line foisted to hoax opposites

purple is successes of a melted grate blanker all
new talk of sachets comparable are wetting
and wresting your face you who the dynamic

reply you care for are they and people some
clips of the time off better swerving not ready
made to be tolerable grease and love echoes

into the steadycam nights weeks you break
off never which sachets delete bar overalls
elsewhere new sneaks run off by heart so

what so far non-nondescript hope agitate
pending several can ready you cry up nothing but
in the end makes your hair and teeth drop out.

AMONG THE GOLDEN SHEAVES

In what upreared assent soever
      smothered frozen linnets
trip and chuck, over and out
      the lay they rent out

no the frosty flurry
      of all arch dissuasion I need
not say does not
      echo or often ease

the strain of a little bill
      by all means necessary
not to amble by
      them not a maudlin retort out

choose this for them
      right little discarder
it makes you hang on
      cue an honest terror of happiness.

THEY OFFER YOU SWEETS

Sun sinks off the coast of Portsmouth. Local bus
                schedules collapse. It is okay
dealing a little smack, the petty
                cash echoes through in beaten
up parkways, like your friend calls you
                up, float a while. No person
should beaten and bleeding cry out, leave
                me alone, I am too young,
the light cast on that is impoverished. Smoke
                is a way of life rises
wishy-washy to zeroes overhead, runs out
                from his flat terrified
childishly that fire could shred it and his visible face,
                do not wish to hurt him
alone you drag misery out, instead cut back
                free their rages blind
them to fire always. And so make the shore too incessant,
                no edgy sea, but
alone the slope low shoved pushed down to a dark
                base, insoluble
garnish of dark sand underneath where
                vision must be defunct.
It is the financial cowardice of a democratic government,
                turns them over, fucks them.

INSOMNIA

With a neat smile, hurry
light up and fashion it dire,
    can you believe what I can
you hear of scrub your sea peer
    sunrise, how sewed in that
disgust into resting even cleaned,
    stoned, there is the same add daytime
ripped by wanks and were shreds
    of it daily you were flinging out
is the truculent teeth rip through sugar,
    no wait, in the car stay
stay your hand, be a drag or, paling.

Or two. Together, we
always remember to say love life. To soar
    bird, to skip off flatter in
to clarified air, as you do but competently.
    Rub our eyes, let rip
in perfect time, on the head nail. Stop
    counting the letters drift,
what we see is a day topped up to carry
    gazes away from
day emptily feasible, should slit into my
    slit my wrist and pick out
from in there, filthied a bright disc.

I dreamt that we were standing
side by side by windows.
   The light there was a lemon blue,
the stop of your head brushes away shadow.
   Drifted poppies on a lawn
you felt for my smile. Now only you could
   see, in its reflection a fresher
taint for that window, a neat seeing,
   throughout a neat colour of rain we count
off its fall. We two stood there together,
   then walked out there, two
feathers as I thought real our first step
   by step into no communism.

COLLECT YOURSELF

That at least is something, rubbing your
face in the truncheoned ice
cream less light is corrupted more accept
more alone, what you

say you are echoes out, a moral chin
yours, scripted flesh-out
when the problem was raised they in
tune were unique opposed

fuck off and brigades of whereas
might say dispassion not
a great deal to pick among could
I even when implore

to separate the dots, the gashed
out tepid fire reasoned
face just a faintly and squatless
that is the door, that is the way.

CUT TO LENGTH REQUIRED

Less excluded through that spark
in you could I thrill must
I keeping on breathe ice out in darkened
habit perpetuate the waste of lust
your life shines, also incomparable
drop to
                smashed me in the knees,
pushed you up against
wanted the money to get high on
glue or free, I now for love famished
will breathe even flattery like
the air loved sex confiscates. Do you
can you catch wind of this, in
this are you lived about likewise
stopped, will you make it
up to yourself through squeeze out
me from your life and again trusting
your life
                again lustful, and in
that trust fly from less excess, to a qualified
cock give your tongue gently and in
turn are loved gently undefied
by now the resist switch, the remote
list of what this life is pinned
to the wind broken down and leaking in
to my throat like a stilt. Do you first
craze for detachable. It starts out you
first then Palestine caressed shouts
and gone in the head, then again
Palestine, then the touch of you resulted.

In the still of adrenaline, the creep of irate
              stars across a clouded tryst
over your head forever, in the farthest
              fetches of intent ambivalence
down upon Idumea, upon pallid Dover,
              where the transcendental synthesis
on standby whirrs on, where additive
              sea butts and sweetly bashes,
a sopping coup for pilchard and sentiment,
              beyond then into the credible heartland
brimstoneless, a rosy haze over
              extinguished pitch heaps, and the streams
thereof in fixed dreams of less
              forgettable amnesia, in the street, here
and/or now, where together we commit this freedom
              a standing order, hereabouts loitering
predicates can shiver, and each looks up like a child,
              and each singly dreams
unagitated, of a job in the Iceland ice-cream sector.

RITALIN DAIQUIRI

I'm as passionate as the next
way I discounted a stab in my forehead
get void of all wiped of all omit
the next way never to break up
and expedite sorrow, then be
alone vague
                        a crisp on
                        ledge by that
do you take the crowd at face
can a fuck glorify and as
tremendous as they are all the related
facts they are blur don't bring
them up one
bring them up one
                        at a time
                        better spent in
you damaged and
rejoins the whole erotic affront
star as yourself in alien bingo
alien washing up little do you
alien alien and later we began all
decreed iron on,
                        heat
                        of you on
me there was a tenderness I
wild to cry for I pick
I did cry broke the body undetachable
was not therefore hateful,
it shone with you keeping my heart
you were keeping my heart
                        you kept
                        warm, there

nowhere the sultry blizzard in
my likes and disowns
spat from you fakes hallucinates spits
from the ground we are can a fuck
waste my time can time waste
my love I ask you everything
                    and this too
                    bang

BY PORCHLIGHT

On the street see: further commerce in hatred
of the waning edge, so they slide
over and grip output slides up nobody has
to do what they don't, want to
                              do you make this plain as day,
were that just window wishing. Plain
as nights also scissor, and centrally our bleeps ping
all switch the mute on, edge out
fashioned by zeroes. It's easy as this: get out while
                              you can radishes
in the egg slots, chaos. The edge can
just be obsolete and not waning and why
not. My retro centrepiece. Only a long, hard stare
she said will pop this zip, switch the finical
                              massacre to gray don't
gape you seem retarded. *As* the news seems
at the edge of my government,
Nigerian pipeline outburst, rain here flushed
slick grimaces away, and every window
                              sill was runny and shines.

SCUNTHORPE MON AMOUR

British Steel today went Dutch my love,
the verbal dead sea won't get me down,
freshly cut the field between trial and
error my whole life can traverse partly,
a small part for most women and men.

The steel of my nerve also is brightly
cashed, stab the mogul. In sullen or
subtle pleasing phrases I show hereby
steely to breaking point, how I outdo them;
trial and error are the climax of this cameo

flesh in the halted turmoil of reasonable
passion for veracity, speeding
despite that halt, in the field as cash.
Suffer a quiet hand to shade your
gaze in its gesture love, for Koninklijke.

DELETES SEX

None too exasperated penis, arise to
the cloud smoked out wire scrubbing device
minced-up fire and lost filed
minutes in dreamt-up oblivion, a throat feeds
this again and again edits wish-lists
                              singular take the very best
                              put first vaseline
don't you tear me like a script. As get drunk,
a way pins and tightens, you that way are
happier caressless shank out, you too bendy
face shoveled on a head. Ironing
bed-sheets, lacquering them as can moonlight,
                              in the way blocked
                              drains keep filthy
rain out and shine alive I press my
teeth through wasted time to your pretty cheek,
caress your ankles and throat, then pull down
steer wheel miss out on collision,
a small melodrama of tarmac and now punctuated
                              face ripped off
                              the cuff you recommend
peace, dialogue, a new end to shot-off mouths
tongue cut by bite-size, too freed
speech slurred out clipped out, our sticker from all
glad use freed, and again the complaint is inevitable and
parallel to the news each propped on the table
                              switch ffwd. anus
                              to heart come in

did erupt like change fails. To happen
at all so the script. A young boy shot in the face by
what right screams. Come on shit-face off
your mind on snorted vanish rattle your
head the biscuit-tin, snap out your throat
                            this more do often
                            would like to see you again
eyes sliced into shelves put then eyes on
these shelves whisk and paste them look at this
proposal to cut tax. It does what it says on
the burnt-out arab lips read out on
the dinnertime news like a joke slurred,
                            in kissing you perfectly,
                            wanting you
to love my face. Sit on like a buckling fence
which won't crack up you crack up
you brush your teeth off you switch off.
I'm not the person I never used to be. Such that
outside, the disillusioned bank sprays cash on
                            so creamy
                            accepted wind licks off
tanker windscreens which all squirm twist orgasm
and yet, are bland. The secret is to delay for
as long as you are. To negotiate a dismay flap,
and the pressed stoical and oh get up cancelled in
to the trash-compactor shouts a debate
                            runs through the grotesque
                            chisel list cut

in toothpaste with a Mars bar. But, we can
make love. And, we make love. For a buck we can make it
leap through a hoop. I from the script hurry to edit out
your breast, feet-paint, beautiful hair-cover,
lust after justice for lips-gear scalpel batter
                              me rip me stop
                              altogether U.S. beating
blood out like your smoky heart. And then she turned,
enunciating: "The procedures of the laboratory
tests render the concealed infection visible
and meaningful to the scopic technologies
of epidemiology and some other bureaucratic
                              surveillance practices.
                              I am not mysterious."

THURSDAY AND FOREVER

The street rate more feasible is cylindric,
continuously the visible subjection fails
to disappear of ourselves to estranged,
mutilated sincerity, as however the backdrop
rises to clinch you hopes thrash about,
I cannot begin to disclaim how most idiotic
wishes I have thin, they screw up like
crepe and easily burn. As faraway I wish
parades through my eye disheartened,
at the petrol stop, that the agreed tremendous
corrugated flight into Parliament should
eradicate you fool, every branch of indirect havoc
gouge out fitting room for the medicated
solid infection you are if too late
discuss that combined anyhow, I see basil
in the windowbox lilts. The storm they
are created passion, people each ran into what
had faced conjecture off and burned this,
twitches, takes back her hand. Could we now
each sees myself descried as always inside
flamboyant neutral bodybag of air and rain,
teeth habitual so face of you, so alert fixate,
so they said the power cut. I cannot believe
that the U.S.A. hadn't provided for this,
sneers at the bang away outside and falls
down time destroyed, where became of
my perfectible love for you, you my
intensity has serenaded that fades, in a corridor
way broken remarks distribute everything,
each cassette of sleep is live, the forensic
regiment of dreadful love and copy

will you base Belgrade on the whole thing
this evening. Wishes flock to across
possibility in a flash of quiet they take
viciously into your buying power and die,
six cloudy feet to the back rubbish.
Pace yourself to the dead centre of that riot,
I reflect on the street edge. And of embraces
such as these now querulous ask nothing.

As life were or were not

      put by distemper inter

mixed beyond claim or

      my correct order, move to

remantle gently; be where

      always and the turn from

always lately gives in

      tact benefit. Still be

lied by life the slight

      purview beside

you says you

      fit throughout, where

finally who knows, is us loved

Mincemeat Seesaw
1999

Fit A

To evade cinereous ice which cut
                back repro were they set
up for retraversing as
                if incomparably or mute her
skips a beat, recall it were the attached
                remit-plaudition to faded
trust to appear refreshed, her for
                skips back put allayed in
stantial, should there ever be
                come back as a choice, now I adore
her will not be remote fast to
                hide which cut
remark that, age of my stray through honey
                suckle and flaring
rayon to put undercut said probate retrans
                mission to sink
a fortune, angelic edicts scattered and bent
                on a rise in fine
mind and clemency set up put tract
                able to sigh scoured fire, wink
out at her, grazing
                her wrists, on ice:

slowly the park is colourless
    it should become that
re-entered way, not and of to begin
    with more to begin with you
should hear say a bent put by, no way were that what just
    inside its own stayed
flare you'll ask to freeze, high vacuum
    conditioning to a crass jot all in
rate-saccharine stop how stop how put
    by does her
the park is flashing does
    her
terror die on in shoved hypo pigeon self-help self left that die
    in vs cash out ab-hypo
respite they should all be alert
    I can see the sea-waves converting
I am torn by a contentless anxiety
    pink and yellow, top end
rasp caving in stop or put by gristle reflac my heart's on
    fire and ice redound
if you may now to her to her now do not stop
    we were pleased with the news

stayed in a received zephyr, fair
zephyr I shall trust shall iron and irresolute
now flickering,
pegged in trust sit to reset no hear out is an honest gale
is screeched famine is too
scorched cuts too pay up too fast
to deny for her
it does all this we see clearly to concur we see pay how
put by, received heed-stack
one to two the rift there thank you within which
fair zephyr, newest rated
zephyr elides with pain, again say and proving anew pay where
a blustering, real famine it is
trust in trust in a rift real rift fair
minded legal fact-attaching here
goes she shall see her terror at her
feet now glazeless daylight floods the sky
I am in love and apprehend the earth do not gain subtlety
you, fair zephire
to zero repay here goes put a wisp of hay register yet another
dying bootless other

started to rain then must get obliged to go
                on to the go on route sallying
rooks at bay they do notice are as contrite too late they notice
                love under the drill, so sunk
base beneath their clatter arrested break off gaze
                up at a rising
sky, levelling
                whisper; to gasp
proof that I am
                to lie is
another lie flan debit mash liability obliged to prevent cabbage stuffed up
                high as the swindled stars can be
are now with just repressive ease, twinkling
                by me as, I ask
break were there storm outside would then say on be proof
                were light on at her heel, advancing
calmly at access recession on in via stay which contrived
                need for a lowest care
could slide and blur down rate super-astro I love you

circa moderate L.E.D. tocsin
utter darkness, all together we had approached in
                saying which I
all together we were stop my mouth
                is full can't were hopeful we
had hoped to approach, to a fanfare
                from a blaze just skipped out had the right turn
over and trust still full over had
                we done this
she asks, I frown at the fireside pane and smoke
                idles out of her
budget alarm break on put wasp-incut by as little
                to do through the playground, the intercepted letter
of the Abbé Guyot on our minds we
                were approaching had
more time did
                choking in enraged
hope stay with us for for
                ever step up money down step
down pay up stop flat:
                I am content with a contentless anxiety,
cobalt and indigo, see the sea-rudders

I, Keston Sutherland, am from the royal dale
                    from here within which we may watch
out at the sleep and dew blitzed
                    weeks one two watch sit as a united put
down to put up with
                    held her to sit at we did it all go on to crouch
at to infer a watch set, no relief
                    for those for whom the taxes are fated
sweat spurting from down in those people
                    do say barbaric seely
lilt of the crossbreeze just where
                    it is in between what you find just
ice and crimes of toy fire convert to a deft plain
                    hope and what time
was it I
                    had better be on
my part
                    I am twice loyal

not cattle at fear deposit here too tautened grades of bright
        pollen see disaffected swaying
out of hand shot pollen see
        not pollen please trust
me too I'm scared
        there is an opening in
is a part of this
        storm put out snapping in
place I was buying
        from a friend I
too part of the destiny
        of fen drainage circa 1641 here
too, here, as I am, not
        cattle not see not put cracked in
pollen-sea gay wave upon: ait
        enim iram esse cupidi
tatem doloris reponendi

here upon peace data to rely
               let your grip drift, down
stream and there to the side not
               idle contrary perfusive there
will be less
               to break
you do you
               hear listen, lapping
there will be less
               we put this
to the executive stayed by a new iron
               reflex and can shift
much as like but
               rust in no peril
I am relying
               just elsewhere on despotic brutism,
as are you,
               ink pig

waved her fingers as he left
through to same pattern wanted too
            much be casual she
whispered goodbye put
            aside for an ambition
there was appeal a precept a by credit-transfer it did
            not fail
her life which
            day speeds by most
gradually would you say by waved emptied
            fingers, for the level
evening, it had run
            as glue in acid his
shadow speeds by and by
            grades dissembles she
stands alone, and in her door
            way is placated, waving
person shut up nothing is not shattered
            less than less
life down flat at hold fast as a spare rung
            set her
eyes run over, as he sped by
            waving back and sighing

                    smear my eyes with oil then waft
          lid up down crack cover my
                    face it matters
          flea-head there's nothing it likes more than not than a
                    rent my throat out
          side there's gnat fission to other people teeth waft
                    up down rot out that is
          her favourite nothing more people you
                    say yes other
          lip snaps up is glossed it matters, too little
                    to lay about better
          moving nothing better she is my favourite
                    lease my tongue she
          is really my pill divides up they are
                    all starving it's
          raining out it what it other you say yes your
                    right in display, sunk
          other flea-head
                    several scraps of drift-food
          head for rent she
                    has a favourite, I shall waft
          it matters my lid up
                    down it's me

with global badger-tetanus and high full with wild
                    roses hangs the
earth in the wind high
                    loves its wonder
collation shut up put out swipe put up temper reset
                    I know what's going on I know what's
going on I know what
                    scrap no excuse, where
are you
                    fusing your snitch stayed what
are your eyes to your repeat hands
                    swiping today goat-dissent
I am in love for the world is a mild shadow, inside
                    which is the way
from itself battery
                    prawn farms on the coast of India
repeat rape nothing
                    much to do
with you
                    boy this or that Wednesday

closed in to what all you liked scant not often,
            came upon a pale face to sync beaten,
all about that tender place no vile thing
            too soon in so soon perishing;
valued in part at large the dream for this,
            tender still may distort at ease those images,
night of my say and say to rest
            that so it may I trust;
the pale face is to wear out love me further,
            notice of my dream by a place one way tender
or the other and still in for retort competent,
            to watch as the police are wept away

Fit B

Sun's up and we're what's breaking out in warmth what's
                    what easily said so
what I heard this sexy Russian free
                    fall batters world market, breezily played
and pliant in the obsolete prolixity
                    of shade and ashen
visages squint it up pack zero dilate do you
                    need more time flash
back with your eye-glint set alert your pegs in
                    to the earth of this premier bio wait I
I see a numb love, at
                    rest at
plodding
                    down
I see a
                    shutting my eyes, I
at war
                    do not disturb
that rag in the ditch which smothered in Tesco
                    own slash-price lo
ving sunray
                    62.7 drop
5,399.5
                    shop til you learn
to stop
                    bogey-boy here from say wank cut cut cut

was a peachy rise in the mock
up net addition to productive
capacity we swam through the air
all night, fixed as a groat
and pelted with kisses to a ploy supple
so far no but hacked out distract renew you
know death is nothing
but a trump splinter of aggregate supply we
streaked throughout the night
straight up put pelted with
all through
the night repeat check pin not
too fast too what no I too
little to make iterative, all through the night
a blessing I am to my own,
only semi IRA,
semi tinned mackerel

On a Jut at the Cape of Good Hope
           cannot yet despise with a baleful
eye too slimfit
           each unresanctioned
shifted inch of to placid
           minds a breathless empire under these waves
each twitch of straw get
           out in time each caw and trill-less
this veto what can
           call it you should prejudice
I cannot yet disburse at a feckless cut
           back repro rate rate what rate rip
grin into place disburse it softens
           there on the incline, inset, in
good time bossing and sobbing can
           not disburse or despise well
what did
           you expect put spun and saw geen
uitgang rook
           verbode put out
I cannot trust I am young I hey plug in connect gust
           to game for a change
of heart at a choice
           of planet slimfit opt-bin
were surveying the daze of drought at the tip of these waves
           which clash and bellow, a rota
dismissed re: circumspect contrition bash up, few scattered
           kids and their life hop
by and berate as
           you may you may
buy your love for them bulk,
           cosmo inverse rehab
say it could be for the choice of nothing new

little pennons on their heads which rotate as they trot
                    Lesotho Lesotho
permanent vacancies positions
                    vacant hinweggegangen I'm
I say I'm I am
                    not to desert put
where mouth is your
                    each component undulation set in
no fever reset scam to perduce I see
                    the sea in ah waves the birds
in sky ah just
                    one second you these
people where stop their bonus stripped
                    softly from their ever restless
positions vacant no
                    rustle no option not
to buy for the ear buy
                    what did I say that's
right,
                    rotate

                    I wanted to capture the whole world,
to be what will coerce
                    and had I failed, had I to want
a drowsy nettle idles wholly
                    ought be more calm were
swimming
                    we free at heart
a day pings out
                    quick burn intermodal connive get
nowhere must
                    stop must I hurt get
set make the whole
                    world captive with your option
but have not turned
                    in time,
did not pick trust did
                    lulling the scraps of attempted patio, we all
wiped out better you
                    said it and say on the nail you fix on
I would like to join in
                    wanted to fail forever

                    so far round and round about
    my love to spare and not lock out,
                    about assignated and can break
    free or bend free once
                    pauseless, always
    then tattery,
                    uh-huh but
    to yet conflagrate in advance pearl-eyed,
                    retort tiny slit exceed,
    and so the swap and sway of flame
                    for flame headed put do sit up
    at denting ice
                    still, if you break you pay,
    still, I'm rubber for fifty points
                    and you get two

a sigh of snow falls in
differently upon my patience I am at
                    rest it's
low in the sky and for this legitimate, frozen in
                    safety from panic
and upon
                    forgetting this I
too a feat of treason
                    new friends London Paris New York
call out to your friends
                    new names go by
so, a sigh of snow falls
                    say a sigh
and all the rebate forecasts are trapped/battered in
                    tonic sobriety taken for
a fat lot of
                    what
it's never not and nor
                    is much else choose this
hook first

a secular upward trend in vapid glee
        as flowers their idle sweets exhale, relays
love to the fathomed packhorse so-and-so,
        the bees drowse out, investment peaks and suds
of gamer prattle spray from washed-out mouths,
        the grace of trended variables to be borne
not of yourselves, nor yet to tease awry
        the flat-out frown and all it militates
in favour of as wrapped in plastic rags
        an Afric baby slender as an elf
sidles in picturesque sedition, in
        time to the beat of the fist in your heart which sprung
open reveals the grip you achieve on love,
        who see fit to lunge at it, timing a gag in the dark

saw the candour dwindle, softly
                whispering upon a flame
wherein of these neither
                abates though both weigh
one gnat and career
                as it may see
it flutter, swaying
                for instance I can see
to it to see saw fear, desire
                ramify pelted upon approach fled out bickering
one put candour one put can shut
                up to a peak of say, candour
sucked and blent in a bin full of wasps
                into summer, and at our liberty
purveyed saw the rapid
                start here
nothing before it's neither
                a lie to abate nor cut
out, what you can
                trembling gently upon candour
must then be beneath you

took the floor shrieked in reply to expunge trust
                        three or
four daubs less
                        horror may
you'll agree be fit
                        idiocy to this end quit
as only you may daily
                        and from one real
moment to the next
                        recant decoy quit/found
out to be sniffing
                        out my heart one
notch to the next and no trust
                        leaked, put I swear
tonic in soft out
                        or burn up to the twinkling sky part
inert and police by-product
                        to soar there vacant
but would I lie
                        down to this end fit in panic out flapping
rebel tongue in chirpy
                        despair through a pint of TFP, moonlight
sloping against the out
                        cast issue of hope
errands as I trust
                        you too shall ape of the total spin

alert in a song view to scattered
confetti to seem remote trot way past
worry no
loss of insight out of sight so seem remote or out see proven
distance flocking in, to forfeit
first lapse in noble annoy too brief
you wail, and let you fall
to stacking the inches
dreadful calamity
wedded to a vow in blue fire, go on put
me out, my love can I ache to
there may not be a revenue
in this alert, busted and tottering
by and down the bend
of a naked street, for a clad proof
taken by
Taiwan by numbers
sing this vow
what can this song vow be

placid gape a friend and sure
                    fire gain in
real love,
                    trundling
up to a high view
                    reject mezzanine (A) to pang out get
together you
                    may
just these seconds
                    or so ago (B) have
leapt to note just
                    this, take a break
Bukharin there is a minibar in my brain
                    and I elect
you by me all
                    brothers to
sisters and back again,
                    otiose rebate faucet
gripping out
                    of the placid ailing question,
weeping (C), hinder this forfeit should you
                    may be happy in
your turn and still
                    the leisure you regret,
outsourced, easy as that

Fit C

That day the rays through cloud racks broke
                in and in time their careless proof
all placed about
                me startled, candid
soft regret even tires to erase this, plain when I ran
                alarmed in a rattle of faded
shade and repression, from a woman,
                stop
I have it both ways
                can she deride this perfectly,
batting lashes coerced crime descriptor
                I will make it all fit
when I ran
                out able and alarmed, battered
out the downward redress autarch static
                fist in the sunlight, both ways
clipped apart and ruses
                spilled at a gutter end,
that day
                and day to day
and daylight
                some day they are permitted

on the face of the season on my way here
                    you may compare them
the face of everything
                    the hazel and white-thorn
sycamore, lime and ash
                    at York, ripe walnuts
bricks
                    percussive softness, within
a mile and broke into fine hills and shadow
                    today it is in the north
clear sunshine but cold
                    but made fresh shoots
and shall continue the best ever
                    their person had not betrayed them
betrayal is far greener
                    with such a year,
and care is odious,
                    vile, though not betrayed

few arid between rain slits open
        called a blank, thereon
set her foot
        Paris was usual so between hot rain by wind
carrier and a dozen
        hostages fried wherever
there was fierce debate, wailing
        back she tore in
half a mind at
        me where
wind quits this quits, later we set back
        to love and withdrew
it with us, over
        a bridge and flew past the lobby to
bed and rode me, softly
        as I would your willing ear
might crave a new world static,
        new breakdown,
newer blackout

were indeed it to be, that free
of my idle dark regress, a shimmering
fall in my power
to stop as
I alone might left
me hurt where every
hurt and every repetition, stung
quick and still
yet here,
and yet brightened, and O were a frail
deceit alone
to bait these, hurt
and repetition which only
fail as a joyous cry
to what was life may disowned in a new
wind raced down through
over flattened tar broke
and happy to the coastline,
where before returning,
and I could hardly
breathe at
point you made
me amazed
and joy so
alone you sent this question, love

             sag along the Milthrop turnpike four
miles straight down
             the lane to left calmness
brightness calmness
             roar of the waters, five miles
saw the forge the Dæmons at work
             by the light of their own true
fire trailed by
             beat into bars and plates
and brightness, calmness
             Burton to Lancaster
news o'erhung
             I even slept to
night in peace despised assuaging
             panic in azure blowtorch wafts put
scattering pallid glisters,
             novel shadows about the wharf-side
but you a little disorder
             in their position
you ad libitum like
             Khayelitsha come no fixed
hysterical
             contrition six
miles five miles up a warm
             and finely dappled
airspace
             analyst warmth/dapple forecast from which
metal may rain out numbered
             as your days yet over
look your hours evade this

as we cannot build to raise are stricken in
                        breath to a novel fire
sound, from trust at my heart
                        it raised, so put can I too cap
my fire with miserable dust
                        as only thus I may calm
now and
                        plainly alive
faggot
                        juice of the pandemic ultra
my little island
                        Ascot bleeding gums
wait for it to crash in
                        and bellow sic recall from
trust bellow said at my
                        heart gag at as
we cannot thus I and cower at sagging slit of dawn
                        rip requited to all acid novel
bland and slender
                        courage to turn in time, all
flash in all always and forever plainly
                        pathetic to fail exhort you

slander fares in a lay
as what her wrist in strip
of lint for the clear and easy shadow
does not fail,
and a break of day from
day so brittle is easy and clear
sleet pale in the vanished driftway
settled and then into a brightened hour
for what good manner of disbelief
quick retraction era or a winter
to sanction for what sudden prick
of guile and scarce flair,
sea-wave, song-blue, sea-change
I sit smoking emptily
I am in love
and love is a militant acceptance,
the daylight in slander of shadow

              for and against celerity
inflow of the magic forest
              don't titter but slap up a list
crossed swiftly what to bounce
              what matter or slip out cast
down or unable to snivel before I fly
              the desire a thrush I
am and need
              a cigarette Congo uranium celery
a wavering chisel a life
              line on line and avidly
sketching a blank should cut
              this out now
and then get proud and aggrieved, to whisper
              to whisper the free
cure of infracted loyalty
              is dearer, or dearer for me
than the self
              catholicon of its obverse velleity

another light show and Israeli avocado
           in the morning my life
is a cunt how are you
           go Chirac go
off the boil as I do
           break my head in out in in sad
soft self deposal for
           what fix of entrained alarms
our heavy our cruise our barrage
           milk it have
a go pinch a line
           their silver coats reflect
the dazzling beams (GAY), the harvest
           scrolls to a blazon icy to
mind as a wood-faced tin
           pot plastic iron willed retort,
from a rubber demon, he only who can say
           fire
ping
           pop
pow
           we must destroy this monopoly, now

this blunt line is a resource sleeted under
                    say did you spend your pastime
nose to the wild flower, to wind
                    up with what left
over in damaged and tossed about by
                    nothing to prate for a bind
gulled to purple year, to yearn
                    up the scavenged
banter accounted for sullen or put by
                    carefully this to remind
broken the pretty ear, not
                    dread too much a real chance out set out
perfectly, I could her
                    hair or what
rusted spade too
                    gannet I could be
trustful now, were florid
                    wild to rise
up to greet for
                    all my spare indifference not too out
of mind tipped but apart
                    so sorry, for what my chance
had settled as, can I be sleeted under,
                    still this is the near blunt cover upon that
and yet run idly I exhort the sea-covert

it is a robust world, and such
a robust earth and not afire, pivoted
nowhere to stare
out magnificently, and with a roaring glaze
at daylight which robustly
inward cannot fall, nor ever shall my heart,
it is too robust were a face
off either to trap in to pincer by, yet my own great
dread should not ever fail, I have far
too nerve for this, it is yet ever rancid default
intransigence and to floods out
far to cheapen real death even laced
in brain with piss-mash not a word breaks
near to even against this I ever will
pivot to stare and collide
with nothing afire, we must never triumph,
you must never either

              put to the floor, which sunk
out and stuttered may so uplifting
              seem and be that truly too, aware
awaits the term to deny this, it's
              you or me and the sun
sets up in a ponderous flash wait for
              ever so quickly and on
what, for what to be finished,
              yet what's more
to come is always fair, hear flutter
              a secret receipt at the grate
no rash jot too late scratched-out I'm bar
              barren fire zero wait do
you see that, and everything must
              go and everything
stays to
              fro or sweetly
swaying between, and yet to stay
              is never either, cannot be put a sea-cut
such piteous jokes and faces passed
              up and away and ahead, to stay
in the rise and fall of the dead.

Poems collected as
[Bar Zero]
2000

A LETTER TO BRITISH AEROSPACE

You were the grand directio more
than a scuffle would surely grasp this,
throughout see the weeklight
come to zero raise your hand now
                and then even, and not how
grasped but how ungrasped it may
itself seem is the startup delusion.
Even-handed I see this,
the screw-up pallor off which snap trashy
                no-hope codes you
snap up at the first commission to sigh,
hope too can be excellent. Though the earth
may on the daily skids tilt
as usual at nothing nothing wraps up
                peace with a grosser
ribbon of pangs than this, that
the question should so slightly run
so coarse an errand, only between hope-codes and no-hope,
itself smoothed and made you will it
                run out or, not and

well who cares. When in New York I ran
inside, when unbusy I aspirin
too much and just run out the coked-up garment
district wow myself blaze-boy
                could chewed up lights
spat stars out. To my heart streets to nowhere
together saw that slid in
and the sky was thin and everywhere magnificent,
thin faces acheless I went blurry,
                you are the bar-zero you eat
everything and later it's dark. As if it

were dark, how could it ever be so, a light
lunch and the grin slots back. We ping.
They're not all like this,
                    I alone was the one so tremendous.
Elsewhere hope runs what a quiet
person may call its quiet course;
tottering round their igloo, now tending
the rise of an adequate fire things
                    we used to call esquimaux whistle.

I love you, this is a voice from zero-bar.
The codes bright, various you may run among,
this includes the fabulous sky over
and the sky made by metal rains
                    a running outtake, and her bright yellow
sun and cerulean stuffed with crab
apples and birdsong served up as dessert.
Were justice a code also. And whatever night
may mean, for sure it
                    can't be the sole other menu item.
I wish you could sleep by my side,
literally all of you. Then we might
wake up at the same time, we bold and each leaping
out from a doze degraded now
                    to habit, with fistfuls of rubber laurel.
Shrimp run through the Pacific. What is
the time now hope-rated, could run off a sparky
derision true and fireless everywhere
washes the sky back to us, the sky you hope on
                    which to put your foot down.

REMARK TO THE WEST WIND

Ring the changes, ring them up,
as the wind in verdict, out from
the sun departed, here throughout
the city runs on faces and windows.

Wind primordial, disordered
asyndeton blowing over
windows and faces, whisper, is this
here remark yet the camp

concentration touching your
invisible acumen? Outringing
in my ears, the serene
brake-screech you might imitate.

LATCHES

You shall be tendering your resignation, pat the debased
        sky at my heels zeroes in,
in a mood-swing on icon of nothing broken;
        birds track throughout it.

They are the fate-codes irate grey and self-denouncing,
        to rubbish as dewy sparkles
underfoot tracks bent and re-bent and go back to themselves,
        and going back with them

you, yesterday my face-coo today all floods and malaria,
        soft taco wednesdays, accepted
words shoved anywhere you. I can say that endless
        regret is that toyish: death etc.

TO THE LAST ANSAPHONE

Beneficent, whose will so slight and even
        yet shiftless by meriting zero must eradicate
                zero and panic would never except
for stunned in the barest gazes clinch on everything,
        this bashed-in is the face I
                too gaze from or at anodyne-face,
and yet zero, yet found by the sleek touch of her
        neck still to be fastened on
                to gro-late auto-craver-me as up top fiery,
repeated, untraffickable outburst goes on razes
        traffic in fire and restates the celestial
                counterpart in a blink and mere daylight.

Beneficent since anything like that
        rhythm of trust or even bashed-in
                greyed preemptive echoes of this turns
no cash midflight, is the 57 channel zero-echo and head on
        any fire to get happiness once somehow
                kissed and my face changed
nothing you see yet wow, what stop brusque
        insta-stop love got stuck
                on my head and lingo got all done-up,
so that a credited passion through I
        think these deadened livid days, seeming
                so wished out may like a soft face brighten.

Lust now merely for what, such as that
        no-one contrives a dead-end and just names
                this the midsequence you skip over
into the sunrise as who did who blinded whom, by what
        news of more stricken I wince I
                cry me vacantly, fill me in whatever did
zero do to deserve this, so to be held up
        over the sedate riot of yes and no are you
                exactly where you are, now,
yes or no, or do in a civil screech we run out pass
        by slip from and feign over
                all the beneficent life unstopping.

A POW ODE

For a second leave it out purposeless
have I a new run verging heart
pounding the floor flat take
me with you cry out a hit current starry
                    fiery burst out, of
mind completely where you step up,
these are my hopes swapping, pan
fixed to nowhere and out: be mine my
be mine worry studded or she star my
                    be fiery as grey burnished
mine this steel to fling over them cut
on by cut she was the driver brown
fields tore by window saw birds up
trance of me pressed on she drivers
                    take me where I lead for
all my life the passion I screen in, how
do we go, on alive crate by
screen in what purposeless they to
be heard storming craze among us
                    one may stand or wait: trust,
what news is called this: what of
it is you proud, you not sorrowing,
claw of sodden tree part the air to drain
free away, over the wild choked
                    sands the wind you suffer
fall little blinks upon you, "dazzling"
"intense" "dynamite" "hilarious" view
birds wheeling upon the stair cloud by
rote bet you don't get all scruffed up turn
                    out the lights kiss
                    serrated she drove me outside

flutter the green, all turning
connive at been prior of all my life I
was a plain follow what you are taken forever,
can that just have been my
                    track forward be mine, would
                    have it so quit
face breaking red blue mirror grey be love
me too much to nip craved blazing done
for spread right over slit on cheer on
were this my error on, and no mirror finds there
                    passion to show and brighten,
                    all of them do naturally,
look at the person you lean: dark
easy noiseless empty bright noisy
easy covered namibian dazzling make a change
made up change that, intense "fabulous"
                    "suspenseful" "steamy"
                    "intelligent" view
settling your queer apart steady see for
fed nothing can ruin me up, tree
hanging over a mile and broke turning
can ruin what of it is you smiling:
                    burn my face off,
                    scratch out to clitoral
swung round you were faintly saying
can be true, whatever all said they do pinching
carried mine off plain away fed
running in of clear doubt ruined driven
                    fields of brown
                    and high lines of clouded
life we stopped and chew breakfast shook
dust from our skins, going by

now forever maybe but hinder
not her but an entire people wasting way
                    later I take
                    my time you can have it
"unmissable" "slick" "fast" "parry"
pity comes at last sews a grasp
on you ferrying in
quickly to or treenight skin or hair driver
                    on time and over
                    all sight, yet nowhere.

Gobsmacked less and less rail in put
out flagrant shining by what you spat
to a token planet and dye
evenly runs upon your teeth upon yesterday
                    upon the streetlife yesterday
young in my scrape, fire in
my way fir under snow and nip out
somewhere above me a hidden trail
to the side blazed, makes run softer lights rubbishy
                    split nail I flung
down on the waving grass in spring,
breeze surmounted, every
thing cops a cut in the price set on
top of the sticker transience has on,
                    so would you make that swayed
for a dash of bronze to pick at: fade
through weeks to fade through, you in
turn they wild are your own
endless Semenovsky Guard of the heart keep
                    on trucking "spectacular"

"epic" "sizzling" "quite" view
I saw her spread a damage so knotted
ends split out to reward in
calm words to strip her off of all that
                    racking my own inelastic
                    give and take your pick:
sun setting mellow crimson, orange
and bright glances rounding
up what shadow fallen
upon yellow grasses they may wane to
                    tonight you are all my own,
                    take from me if I hear
you correctly yelp on, fire: brink
to brink and day, today I see so plainly too
stop turning insight out, what world
may over that clay paste its spell
                    far and writ wild,
                    strip me of my passion up closest,
who can snap contrary yet brink
stutter away who's a happy clay then on
on crab paste sit retching
put on quick the passion in you screen
                    february "human"
                    "blinding" "magical"
"trot" view lately the glamour you were
sprung from caramel tint
to memory has it go fun often you
want to put that back in and go away,
                    but you never will,
                    I'd say if I were you happy

happy as nettles cluttered under pylons,
can my shrug dick out fat change me
the place we would be happy in
is a place in happy hands: view it,
               first with your branded eye,
               coming up next, Xena the gay bat.

Sighing, having, breaching, rank coded
glimpses eyeing the world up, one
can be on top of another
another day flipped to which peep lurching
               did you see I
               cried we all must change,
we must be changed short
breaths catch on spirited
why over persistent maniac dream fire
grate out sorbet to drooled
               to be given freely
               spin or head needed: flag
curving prettily, fluttering by bellowed
verb strings pranking
it to shreds it falls to blankly whomever
blankly you put it on loves you too
               far away where the sun is rising
               light to gather my
profit to see in talented "moving"
"generous" "classic" "dark" view by zero
hazel and currant whack anti and to die
for and sit and blow your top
               rap on her grille
               reach for the star in

livid night detained slid rose and scraped off
hit in the gut's eye by every
subtle season famishing the scum far
tacky but boy did we gaze sing and are wild
                    what can I do,
                    who am I to say quietly,
do I whisper for all of us, the land
sparing my life and fading
heart, will scrawl another jissom
on the desert sand in gore you
                    should be prouder, have a go art
                    curry to fart by
fuck off get your own ideas anyhow
as we were driving right, in nowhere
shone as it could my fashion
of crying out for brightness we both see it,
                    over and done
                    with your permission
cowered and paled where am suddenly
I where do we scoot paled
see you later must be off your mind
flung far again pricks another blink up
                    sun catches the screen fiercely,
                    I will not sway or dream
that you pull over, tree to claw
into shadow a trap we sleep and wake up
in the world clawing
back from garbage hyperion do sever us
                    go for the car
                    or open your trap "non-stop"

"radical" "honest" "Burma" view
cut: the word here is pow,
experience flashes out with it from us,
half the time I leaning to chuck it out
                    is intimate as the echo of too briny,
                    too far wasted, too plain as day side,
trying to hold that the tightened
crate you wholly are vividly to fire
a shadow craving shadows to blend by,
fire makes your stand flattened shadow.

SHADES OF GRAY FIRE

Where are the crazes, where the mass out
running of needlessness,
who disobeys the order break free
always and wows you thin

lifed as you are then less then
turned to fizzy syrup breakthrough, there you
go over the same delays have
that extinct panic, stay straight-faced,

for summer clothes that pack like a dream,
for a new approach to nowhere else,
with soft seditious rains and the idle
urge to give a shit or two or else

and the order is barked melopop
oil fails somewhat, is beyond
the rainbow these flagrant shades of gray
were damages faces,

then should I lonely watch them out,
but the damages are craze
control run by remote fact-pushers on you
me and the speech we

breathe deeply alive, stop you don't
slip out we can always lift those
shades and a finger each at the sky orgasming,
gray ablaze, our faces fumes and echoes.

THE CODE FOR ICE

The patch sewn so well anywhere,
due to the relaxed power of insight out washes
and about news to me turbid drip, I was just
saying due to relax echo, inside
                flip and going sour, get in,
get in me sour, how we can ask credit
our mutter banging out, from the earth back
to front to have flat-out earth on autofire,
fuck you once more drearily scanned
                     gazing, side to
side long vanished I scatter, get the
hell out I once, more say, say what
ever you feel can, loud and clean
daylight is a blindfold
                  RE: further
democratic reforms and political
stability in entrants; improve burden
sharing; increase weapon sales;
dearest light of day you ever
                     burn the powered grays
of night to bright crap, here summer is
here again run away me
throw pass up the canderel serrated, better
off than malawi you were kind
                  of tired everyone hurts sometimes,
don't they RE: cost savings from scale
economies in weapons production;
foster collective defense capabilities;
adapt to post-Cold War environment;
                     croon of her traits and winning eye
lash and of my fire to scrawl set out
breath on alert 2. trap a clarified

angle on time see doubt for the shattered
choir it were, unharmed
                              threw the blind down, 3. you
see ice incompletely scolded won't run
through the proper surges
you bash in that glaze in havoc or absolutely
not you at all don't bash, fetching
                              coy the deleted sparks
they shone and are precisely due, everything
must go yet you stick
around, for just one night the perimeter
frozen and pale, is of
                              yourself too sure as day's
plain and can, forget it
RE: interoperability, can this one hour
flow within our fists spread can
fire be pretty shut, can we see
                              the flinch of our ice wrung.

The code does not treat of elements,
my lips are sleetless, torn
cornetto wrappers stick around idly,
daylight bends up on raspberry creosote,
                              see just how far
mind that you do, time pops
a clatter of canaries arcs off on mute strap
in love, strap in the light of day pat
the puppy sucks the twix
                              freedom is beautiful
twilight ferrying stars to Iraqi
skies in metal descant,

fresh from booth, box and tick
pick a prayer they have
                    the flurry of verbs set free
I carried out openly re. parties will develop
separately and jointly their
ability to resist armed attacks; parties
will promote well-being by
                    encouraging economic collaboration;
on the bruise, an ice-pack; parties
can request that members consult to review
traits check eye check
told me a tale went something like,
                    pleasure to pleasure passes
and the night in grays, new
colours banishing, washes the sight
free, and parity shadowed you
once more can require love
                    yet, free is itself a code
dirt-suffering, you eat the beyond,
outbreak of inner trembling
scruffy face, reek of freedom outcodes
basic ice and click up a Jap
                    schoolgirl branded hot.

Wasps sting a baby and money weeps
O ode of mine you're a diamond,
the cheeks pinching, rubbish
scarlet, try to remain completely visible
                    do I want pee
go-go Honduras in PVC racked
racket of intro, swarms to the beyond

sudden alight, piece by
pieces all the news and I singing
                    into my heart take
I am alone scrap, to worms a pander
flesh careering or
stand tight and sew the patch
of outrage to a hole above
                    my chin dreams are coming true
freedom is not the code; love
free of ice is
of ice, belonging passionately,
you can say free this free that of
                    ice, so what
you say can and will be used
up burned like patent styro cutback
flaring to zero, natter
swung a balloon at sheet eggshell
                    sex on the beach
and love on the blink, things are hotting
up like the fuse in a fridge plug;
the heart gripped like spam by batter;
likeness was a trick we clapped for
                    eye snare, spoon
fed freestyle, to do as we pleasant
shifts in the theatric log may,
but my pain is real hard
and the kid in me split, vector
                    autoregressive techno
staring blankly confirmed that;
politically attractive crisis management
confirmed that; underdeterrence confirmed

that; fire is not the code
                    either; free of
fire we just bite pork scratchings,
watch as the sun sets, gay
fantasies and get a spite on and drool
on fiery drool, it will always run
                    you as if
you ever were caps and bangers, were
cartwheels and a toast, fire,
do you see by its light, will never melt this ice;
spiritless snap of day will not melt it; it is
                    sea-code, metal fleer
of no oblivion, the canter of tanks
to retch by, cost of the price you touching fix,
looks upon us bumped off, torn by
winks the day that's frozen won't run out:
                    your face is not beautiful.

MY DELICACY

The fashions I behave in they do crank for better
        reasons or better still do crank out where nothing
                else that I know could, a world bright and particular,
viewless yellows also myriad, daylight prompt to
        the ear also gannet-face recon of U.S. cash dryads,
                bright everywhere and the swindle of trust a discard,
better still pushing from the lung out through
        fascinated crowds also myriad and all ratified startling,
                particular as they object in fast anger to what still
without fear at last thinning they are my fashions can
        take as a brightening start of redo paradise
                its echo from mouths stringently agape, blushes

are what pink I was seen as, scrape also onto my decor bright and
        signal snapping down, breaking down, to my fashions
                bright world and lung as fast love-icon by
now could I not have changed it or yet
        week to week and dryads sparkle bright in everywhere,
                Bangladeshi newsprint parasols, you are
promised first look-in I know certainty is bright only
        since I love you I we cut just about
                everywhere our losses we jot are startling and ratified,
only we are, prompt daylight never out so scavenges
        a racket of softer regrets than these we say so, from us
                tipping upon the world, dark and so inspecific.

TO ANDREA

Over the shattered sleet there could
you see it drifts in part
intimately, in part withholding
light by a great windless deal
turned trance of the air,
nothing you ever see to daily,
but hope too sees
                    flicked on the t.v. car
window came down electrically
and I am a man in certain love with you,
frightened by myself, eat rubbish
plucked in Israel speed so crushes out
weariness you could again blink
quick, if you want to,
                    that light was
not then so delinquent,
touched upon your face without
invention because yes and no or, remaining
where you are you
are in part the whole of my world
flooded by brilliancy, also you depart.

REFUTED EROS

Glances intensely upon you riot is not
that something you dream for
often and it makes the type
               of you drop, no inflicted echo
               am I runny
and slurred talk that way vitiated so
suddenly to grab faces, to clutch at an eye,
here says you defect luminously, the starfall
               acid to candour. Am I
               dreaming until
now of you put your hand now out
of touch here on me, and grip you breakaway
flame infatuous my head,
               my heart spunks zeroes
               tip into nowhere.

When can that riot go drab,
can the inside spin dry, who were that
faces deceit can you run through
               calmed a sky at 6 p.m. and soft orange,
               often a sun setting,
plaster upon you. Breath breaks from your lips away.
That anarchy of the loose eye
ever should end, yet how plainly can it end,
               neither cuts you up
               loosens your face bunches
of you drop, the shadow that you know.
Love is the near echo
recedes from nowhere, when you said that was a schismatic
               brilliancy outflung,
               were you a thrill of glances?

The wish is bar-zero passionate, it can remain
of itself dark, is the switch of
flinches into unreadiness, exactly the wish is here
            to be without
                loss, lost utterly.
So how do we make compliance a good thrill,
a gray query, best shadowed by
someday by later and by
                riot of your eyelid
                breaks a view in many slats out,
what do they change. Can you, scraping
ease into my ass repair that flinches
turns away. Into dissent and magisterial airway,
                into a rented epos free
                of glances intensely, futile.

ZEROES GALORE

The zeroes count, much more than you think
you don't think and say fuck it. So the beaten
path like an egg beaten is indistinct, what
parts once defined are, you are now
shuddering under the steel cry fork swept across
porcelain you eaten, teeth set on edge of zero.

I feel the world there. Which one mangled
Arab had co-produced but zeroes
you see and maniacs, one or the other has to go,
and fire may yet often be amorous,
the parts of its illustration used aptly, we have
the credit to say distinct things (if not

ever to be them). Zeroes also mean jobs.
To descry in each passing face the one beaten face,
owns no zeroes except ones seen passionately,
what could this consciousness rise up
to annihilate in fatal and glorious sunlight,
by love bound together, the expugnation of all fire.

And by cubicles kept apart, given a free say-so
please leave a message, where did the days
go wrong we tend to ourselves and zero.
The eidetic cutback is moral: a new car in the first
place is too fast. Secondly we throw you
and I ourselves out wildly, drive the night sane.

Where should we go, zeroing in on fire, numb
faced and by that hated fact so brilliantly outshone,
so far well, nowhere. There are a few
odd billion zeroes more, or less autonomous
men in the Iraqi corpse-oil-and-sand-pit. A zero
tolerance state inverted in The Arts, that shrinking

crescendo the light renounces I can't
touch and wake you up myself flickering in
and out with my vague face singing a part
never can be everything, were zero you the one
beaten face perfectly one part one
sky returned fireless anything more than

one death for everyone, finally you
might end, and our requiems then starts reversible and
lovely and the hope won't also end, I never shall.
A stupid gun laughs in a woman's face
fire contorts her, it is a way of letting hope be just
someday and its cold light stacked up in zeroes.

ATONEMENT

                              Turn your head
against a face spoiling, despoil
               adequately sleet and thrashes of light
may claim you
                              fast broke the star down,
rubble of brightness about you, faces about
               you too, as they break affinity
shines, it is your own fire
                                        too is your own and everywhere
they are you solicit
               broad day, entire scission and echoed
silence changes hands

               into icons. What passes for
weeks between them wrecks you,
                              Bolivia. Shines in the mind
crispy, a shiver of faces throws
               upon you shadow, bright urban lattice
adrift among glances like drapery, can you go
                              on fire says. There is no adequate
remorse or adequate reason why
               there is none. Cocaine in the broken home counties,
the pulp of a shredded map left out
                              in the rain you slow
down quick you

takes you for dinner. What are you.
Is this brightness yours, the solicited star
        breakdown also a wet easy glance proliferates,
were an atomic arc that
                overt yet shaped immensely
to the earth as demo fidgets and small fry, would you
        trust me says face to face,
switch the light on, chop up the liquorice and peanuts,
                we belong together.
To whom. As now, across the celestial equator,
        Venus breaks, the resolve and
you are bound, to recast down a faultless star.

A BINGO HALL RIOT

Make this the impossible coup my head is
a coop in which things scar pulp
ditto beneath trimmed ozone, of justice the new
effaced de facto proposition, not cling
not discarded amid brilliant hates you bins,
amiss inchoate c/o a vague rip-down
swing to the vox hideous popped speech
bubble in felicitous steel. Thick as
the galaxy with stars, cold as the wane-free
mission of flammable air, this person
makes lives a script mortuary he shot
you on location glances reel to
                                reel from
him into the emergency vision stash, in
                          which again freed I reel
out ways to be calm, to be angry, to be my gapeless
self a resort tongue at last seditious default,
making the sedate cap on inconvenience
thrown-up as ever before and so reconstellate.
               America will remain very much
                     ditto you hear
             engaged in the Middle East I will
                    ditto you see
            expect it to be a major priority
                   ditto no evil
          of mine and of the department.
                    Also sprach der Öltanker.
On my desk by tomorrow morning rosy
forefinger and index shoved up
riotously at his face: yet give room over
to the convert to unarousal blasé speak up,
let the heart pimp blood out, all talk

of him is minty as rhyme, of him,
of him is gritty jingo against the gag's inside,
the okay outcry strapped on

                                  loosened yet this fire
does roast my peanuts, pick up the cheque go
home like a smokescreen stub yourself out. As I
walked the walk slid but half

                                the world must
bear him company, be kicked-in transparent like
ice on which to zoom and split my legs,
ridded and me eulogic roll-call boy tinpot head,
ousting the scavenged news print-out. We can get

                                  together and
and change that and search for rule
explains of training instances a part, and recursively
conquer examples, blind

                                faith in vitro
smashed outlet, my shit old window buried in
smears and dead wasps. Alone, ready
to look furtive, outside the bingo hall, and crowded
in and wasting away and that sucks.

Wasting away part two: herein the polemic
through use of special language is made enigmatic.
A learning face can thus be characterized
with the biases it employs. I hate you
predict, configured rat speechless intern
fabulously with the fabulous riot colludes,
presenting you played out in-ditto. Past all
body trends hate to caressed dispassion through
time is defined by its hypothesis language

drinks paintstripper. Can we talk about what we
can hate, indict can filament of fury can or
the purity subroutine bounced, struck on
you too dismiss bent my
                                    face it's like
a target concept, top-down search of
the inner while-loop bent I fucking hate
you. Lipstick. Syria. The commercial
break in a Gerron flick your face, love is
knowing whenever can't top laugh top
night scalpelled bin up, aqueous she for
once I'll bet loves my
                                    this decree
slid out decision lists, quiet and
very alone, very
                                    in regression rules
call that in, bingo. Ashcroft might just die,
sooner than we do the trap leapt
in at the prismatic zero-slit it found. This put less
abstractly like yourself you heard it all before and sick
and tired and eager for more contd.
The search space for a learning algorithm is
defined by the heart very amazed, very
sit down and shut up. The while-loop butter
down. Hate is too great a burden to bear
quietly, or as here in a tantrum hated
likewise fashionably echoing hatred. No far-off
irritant like the present, no such luck trapped
easily from myself, as the bullet-points
stanch no inward cataract or face excised, there are
no true panics against this hate which
thus expressed lilts, takes you for

rides on the blancmange-pink mare nowhere.
                              We must always ensure that
                                        put honeycomb ice
                              Israel lives in freedom and
                                        in a plastic bag
                              security and peace but at
                                        and chuck it on the bonfire
                              the same time Arab etc.

Such bitter mint partitioning this air
space tongue-fanned between screw-in incisors.
What could pass for the symbol of flight
in precision nowhere cast in glued-in,
bright happiness in you smothered,
is the audacious prevention of escape so ill possible
and advised, so they
                              say the magic
decree rescripting love you too amusingly
cannot be more succinct. Running on borrowed
crap through costume dramas like a cop in
drag your ear screening you wait wait
anyone may inhabit this proposition and be star
struck happy erroneous and okay. Beaten
up was it, okay. The wind on mashed
potato like gravy beneath the lifted bin-lid, next oil on
toast and my flammable eye rolls over; put
lyrically you might say there were scores
of adamant leers tossed out like confetti. The ears
are anyhow not otherwise accessible to good
sounds than to bad ones or frozen
                              do paint-cans rip up

easily shoves that upon her face are wrong
are in the wrong outright surmised, impossible
runway staggering to a blur,
                                        instead drilled-in
alone with the plastic-wrap and breathing.
Inside you there are chances to crush this man,
chances that prevent your happiness, whereas into
the patent and echoless void we are
the precise muck crushed in, our codified
outrage in the greased spittoon by thought-out
analogue is a torn neck. Wait listen as
quick-wilted possible to
                                        numbers Ion called out
get each one possible, shout out your
memory is easy and I am defiant. Pick that
vision of shrapnel off her, just like a defunct scab,
medical insurance of the radical imagination, and this
imagination cannot be dumped off, ripped off
or properly be fragile, our dreamy ice-infarct up shatterproof,
a discriminated milkshake, it cannot
in fact be fragile while so patently ours,
packed-in with miseries like chip styrofoam.
                        They are going to have to live
                                    I love you
                        with each other and hopefully
                                        so much pinkie but you can't
                        in the near future we can find
                                        do that on the sidewalk
                        ways that they cannot.

EJECTOR VACUA AXLE

For the survey launder nothing phlegmatic.
Foam flourishing out the mouth douses ice,
corners it, isolates it it puts
it out mutes it. A burnt question is nailed on.
Is this written too soon, should there be
more time for hatred to wane first,
for mourning to be allocated, to stop at
all where directed, re-own our desire to breathe
children beneath rock. But I won't
stop I lust like a sickened invert
gluey teeth sprout in this, is meted-out
platter of faces on a screenshot,
held like treasures of the deep contempt
for death which asphyxiates air, death
which way next, to extort from the vacant
sky a smash-up and roll into
the barrack mall, the next rational bout.
The next choice switch along is justice.
The freedom to spend is a defrosted asset.
                              Does this
chat-up line sicken you, take
                    pisses wherever
        cut down
                         ask me a question
sleaze-eyed and rubble-mouthed
to agree with the minister that life has sacrosanct
components and we better grab a few
before they sell out, as the counterproposing
dropped-out heads in a heroin blur
all glitz up the street with their dreams.
Socialism will disconnect a palate from sick.
Bread and plastic robot-penises coalesce.

Take your sliced-open plasticine eyeball and
                    what's the point
                    crying out like snapped-up poor fish
                    tanks sunny
in the mammal way cash acts, defend this way
of life way off the brutality and sex scale, credit
                              lizard
the thrill of an incorruptible love in
this arm. This arm is now around your head,
before rising to sleep you have this arm
with you, tender its fingers stroke off
temerity and insects from your face,
crass light gets stung out or wiped out—was in there
                    just closet the
                    warped astro-bar tout in
                    cabbage
diamond,
                    war is a principle of nature
you wake tight, onerous cloud thickens over
a snapped tooth-reel. Do not get out of your car.
Dream about this. You can laugh all you
like very happily, the knuckles are all foam-white
meat cabinet, recant all you
                         dispatches a blow-kiss to
the proposed exit wound. What would you do if
some crazy Arab smashed your children's head.

                    As the planetary
          spin made by punitive calm in endless
          digits scrolls into endless sickness, to be
          sickened, to have been sickened, the mental

sick-bag production line flourishes like
so in the sovereignty of liberal economics

We are permitted to endure this. We endure
it blank, tin. Reconciliation beautifies pig shit.
Each vote stuffed in a box counts. After all what
else can he do, no government can be expected
not to respond to systematic brutality. Outside
glad severed hands leap about and salute
and veils from the faces of women are shredded,
hot codeine chars in through the sleeping bag.
We would so lose all credibility if not thrower bomb.
The pretense of events includes also an apache
                                    rotor see from
which fire sprung and ripped heads off.
Swept up wind on hill tantamount to a screw-in
palate designates the hope for a speech replica
bongo noise. Romanticism. Nothing
you are stops
                    this and
                    that is a tree packed
                    look birds
collapses or, meat. Smash open the alarm shop.
That children has a black eye. White House
Commission on Aviation Safety And Security,
Final Report Feb. 12 1997: we are all now
the small minority about whom we do not
know enough and who merit additional
attention. Correct this deficit and disorder life.
Do then not disorder life. This one. Automated
hope profiling glistens in your eyes,
a vision of love for our partners in their desiccation

trash heap flashes across the pair, streaks out
of the mind in implicit proof of embargo: zap-cancel
gut red, saw up a donkey,
                                    recapitulate
                    a hold on life,
                    barraged through a slit by visage
                    chaos ironed to
such a replete sheen, an amassed fling of irate presets
news in indelible snack form heads
with the laughter duct ripped wide, do you think
ever. That this margin coerced to flipside
temper fits and religious despair pales, next to
you walk in the street. I take the bike
down, subsequently we reverse this. Going
on with and
                    valuing not cracking to
                    to strict bits this
                    sick love frozen to a crisp,
                    asset sunset.

Would so not be credible unless reactor bomb
shift them with the flush break their
legs advertise discriminating gun hardware shin
brûlée shin-oil, extradite the dinner you
ate to a virgin bag. This is the requirement
to live as a conscript to indifference,
throwing violent words against their own edges
wrappers, twisted bogus in intense felt
sorrow over that obligation. Throw them at the
pink which grass isn't. At ash string
along that gut reflex, the whole deictic

pose lubricated into a kind of hate-crime pathos
extradite the cat-flap,
                              so you're either with
                              or
                              and bandages its
torn with a flag. Correct this pose with data:
institute a revival of also non-sick pointing:
twenty-five Afghans per day are cremated by
Russian mines left scattered among their rubbish
dump homes, milk
                              haircut, new bag
                  glaze,
                              this is a war on terror
and it affects all of us. It is not America
which was attacked on the 11th September,
we should each expect reality. Remember
you how you eat. Who loves you most of all.

DIPLOMATICA FIDES

Throat instigates air, instruct too now to
fall open your eyes wasps fly out
since I will lose myself, and not replaced by
idiot life shrink of discord bow,
scrape and rearrange my face into the same
the same light different panic noted detox
error lost too
                            away from too
                            far my life
in which goes like,
                            you cunt divagated,
                            you sling head,
these my reductions slurred down
caresses like iced, this is the prize narrative
mattering on you die. Of my loss my
you continue bricked in to scream laughing
fast enough keeps fly out. Tooth
keeps cracked on, is life the kind
of accident distract to the base not outcome
bag, flutters across linoleum, not then
in you dropping. Fashion an impossibility,
            make that in shaped,
                            introduce then an outcome
            then annul bar,
                            busied affect heat,
wake up with an incredible list of jobs
stare at the window. The depravity of American
kindness a chainsawed head, in the bar we saw
through the illegality of real kindness
a smashed bulb at the end tunnel come out

seized my face hands,
                love provides this echoing
                flesh end and
is gone how was your light
                reversal also I was nowhere
less where I am. No but Genoa. Where
to next you plum divagated. Formerly the
attached clause signaling political retry added
on became an elegiac shadow, to part
life reconciled negatively, but now even
the flush ascetic ride into discord banishes
itself to the piss-end of the brain,
                gob drops adequately mint,
                the night then spun it witless,
compactor hat a riotous success runaway
life magnanimous like the shallow end.
Bricked all over radish not irreparable end.

Came Theodoric, came Vanish. They do
not caresses iced break-out intractable in
you can, not less stupid than a fringe
benefit locked to rips, distorts too calms
eaten. I shave my jaw,
                have a mouth I shitted
              away park
        by the line look at me there is
              there all that
time left shared exact sic you. Get up and
proceed day. From the total life related
meaning first comes, invisible now to cross each
barrier still this is it dread and gone

loving, blued-out flashes across the spoil air,
the future obsolescence of mere dream,
      alright you can make the
      slide-panel and shut
      door on fingers then by
            kiln
            reposition
            do bar
pulled over halt. Snap a brick in two. Like
that you waste out sublimated pink, trying
on a credo more excitingly reducible
life into it. Our lips merged, sunburned
arm and back, brilliant the taste of salt gag
twist and stare up at the water surface
elastic in the chaos of sunlight, can you grab
floor with her fingers push through
sand ending what
            look again out of the window,
            clouds underneath at
      the tires shred across distort,
      this is how debated continuity shows
thrashed of you, and the desire for
loved community could ripple as a glass seat belt
tongue clingwrapped, a slide and swing, in love
            bag, in
            a catchy time okay,
            then switch on.
            Then switch off.

So ends this action like a spilled brick
non-discretionary, pacific reset out to animate

traipsing birds and the sky below
par blued-out and associated findings in now rubbished
clip life. 'Nearly Always' prevent that
incidentally then crack out go. Put the next
one on now, coincide. 'Sometimes' is in that
rush of the fraught

        no pack of ice bar

        draw-bar

        incandescence of idle sat

pretty alone dream recycle on you of
you beautiful astonish rip, tear out and
situate detested life elsewhere go. At the bargain
shadow bin you can get coffee. Reverse,

        except, remain.

        Put on

the next one now inside good time. 'Rarely'

        is it here

        Andrea you possess

life at the filled limit shining, as abrupt
called out from doubts filthy tractable if
so then bogus, is it ruin to star
in panached self-injury then to cauterize hatred
or blind and bland eat you

        contorts the adrenaline like milk stops,

        running away and piling

up in the shredder now dysfunctional temporarily.
Retaining the ice hack air calmly wrong.
What's the defection rate in soap.
We could now situate "Asclepius at -179°" which on
inspection (philological) would turn out
to be something about cryonics. Does in slur

pow contd. egg-slice by flashes etc. You have to
                    pick one of the three;
                    choose from these the top
                    three most relevant;
staggered by the abject happiness which is
all their proposition;
to the back teeth and parrot land. Spun then
in her chair like a child and now also. Yet,
waiting, as through the what-slotted dark
                    famine or other
necessitated description of true zero I too
much flung am in attendance hopeless in
alive, be too screw-in. Beautiful that
                    harasses the pink like scars
                    you too make
                    resurfacing
depth-charged in butterfly consumerism out
slip of the mind. Help me. I love you this
                    way, this
                    much less
            by zero than possible in fault shines
            the answer steeled out. Now can
            we say that the bricks can has
            already chosen the main link of
            the collective-farm movement in the
            system of collective farm development,
yes we bricks can and should say that
can, main link, pineal cycle lane outtrafficked,
desperately I want to kiss your clitoris
rundown, who benefits by this
                    stupid and harmful precipitancy
                    throwback to
finish as a callous tongue might puncture ice,

no c/o your life, inhesitant
                    too fireflies, at
                    the credulity of death stand
                    bargaining
                    set empty the chairs on
which she sat. Read then about the retreat of
My Welfare State; in vague situate just
the blue outline of an attitudinal cluster analysis,
warping to green in sunlight, defined then
face mine let out extremeless plays zero-sea,
                    then fixed water;
                    sung then air gently bandaged;
                    trees kept on;
contributory to the brick-star go failed demur
go slide into adamant
go escape rushed to the possibility
a healed scream far into faceless output yourself
shine elsewhere alive, in terror of
this and irreducible love I love you torn
up photo-finish scraps everywhere forever go.

THE RICTUS FLAG
2003

EXTREME SWEET

When did our joint faction against each
other split into this mess, cast about
every day for answers to that sex
question riveting us to indifference.
Your peculiarity reduced. Thick with
sex-knots a scab of hair clapped you on.

Passengers on the London train out
the window gravel and paint
tired. Sex is disclosed you took
up the converted hamper flipping
its pointless lock open. I can't sit
and long desperately for you alone.

Instead of ropes the descent in
autumn from the trees belongs
to leaves agitated by our rapacity,
by any exit. Throw your legs open.
Heartless blood in the wind, thin
spaced eyelashes and cars,

tossed there and all glassier than bat
breath on your mirror. It figures that
we fail and come out of it sex
first through the collided, straight
edged coalescence of sanity and
wait alone. There are other ways.

Bins gyrate at the threshold not there piloting
steel spun to a feather cops out. Event
crash to your obliged knee, fillet this
event bold on slit-neck, for lust to flap down
cringe now
                        excites my
                        block of concrete drops
the quinquennial Panathenaic
event nothing. Everyone from Manolo Blahnik to Ravel
via Pied a Terre is peddling at least four
inches of extra lift. Scribbled on
this neck that
                        bin catches as
                        it drops celibate the gears
shift and we fly, snowdrift panics against
the windscreen event hollow tar
yours in, mine also and lured brightening in
hours to collapse like splints I
fake the shadow in my mouth cry or palliate
                        float or
                        was all remunerated viciously,
the positioned snow-bolt clip drop-out
event fascinating and real. Say nothing
happens and the days waste up you prettify
cough your knees out not
remove inner core through front slot
                        —same. But,
                        with the electrons unionized,
fate bent on tongue-ionamines, a fountain
of smoke rakes through, bit-necked
altruism under the stars weigh up chitin on

event speech blackout. You are as
such precise in having gone to die event peed.

Wiped off punched in the throat code all
time you stared at me the
pretend data of extravagant passion veers,
ice-crusted beneath bone-floe,
wings flip above,

                a sauce sprayed
                on your mouth it off
wiper-eye shuttling a cringe vases
these sockets. To undress in the dark
split hour runny under my finger
and work into you, lips pieced-up torn sticker-edge,
seen how we arrived

                like a flight
                of peanuts shuttling to mars
no costed erotic grow-bag, that wraps that
leg in hers. My mother smashed up my painted
soldiers on the coffee table was drunk. I
cut up the cigarette in her mouth. Had to drive
your car home. The wipers

                time you put me in
                closet eat
sand parched careering you blade-head,
the exact cut strung above an issue
an extravagant appeal messy is branchless
ash and leafless is and, when
I love you oceans collapse meat sings,

                shrill to the dead edge and
                planed crow.

A root picks up. Militias parade through
broken residences whipping up the formerly
loyal humans to a replacement loyalty,
jubilant spare parts. They say the colours
you wear snap. As, event caught billowing
                              lash on fantasized
                              film, and matched grin.

Onset double life. Neck switches to wiper
the wrist pleads, cripples a benign blade
sift through focus on the slide. Laid-off
mortar cascades on poached life, you restore
the water supply and the sun's literacy. Way
                              out of line do oil
                              completely the cement hinge,
ghosts trip upon ice-rinks not tangled-up,
their mothers wipe their runny chins. Eyes
the event up. Where does come into
it that you a pop bangs out. Jubilant, happy
aroused people. No blag exists, no
                              say what again,
                              knelt,
I had to realize the extent of her intrusive
absence to hate incorrectly my own life
running up a massacre of panic so self
destructive I could have left it alone. My mother
had her own life. Fix everything. To
                              undress you
                              faltering next a bulb spits

light-like too muck. Nothing is drab
permanently save the injunction to gas death
away in futile self-remonstrance, not
futile enough now change when I was a boy
sticking a carrot in me. Get that through
                        kissing toilet seats—eye
                        drift over the
picture voids caricature, event the rind
fell in possessive ways down
and on the heads as we got soaked through
in a dream you where, tangling at
desperate speed everything you could wish against
                        to slash desperately rip
                        it apart and fitting screw it out.

ODE : WHAT YOU DO

1.

What is death? It is the summation
statement of generations of prejudicial vote.
Dirt polishes up pretty good.

Extrude lust as a monofilament.
Provide in this sunken calibre its limpness,
memory, stick to—ice fries

spattering on, kicked-out then you braid
multiple small extruded, go
all tear-open like nobody's throat.

Point evacuate them, mean the sky
and snow-stars. Eros permits
this, Sabra and Shatila thread through

love they are a polyglactin of
areas unused in the lung.
The ring of fire shines and divorces.

2.

Depressed the contrast switch, flew about you
which make? The autologous tissue snaps
replicates gel bollocks your head falls off.

Both sides of the vicryl too heal up point
the sky out. Its across-centre evocate at
snappy prolonged wind—this terrifying, and

correction no-one. I don't walk to the
bus stop, next I don't commit steel wish
they would shut up disgustingly break

up the tree, steel-features couldn't put it—he
hides and then buries his face. Burns
of evoked light too screech across the leg

cloud in that sky, polished beneath Seroxat,
across the leg that cloud. You manipulate
point defects in a flipper of liquid ash break.

3.

Appropriate life is shredded in dreams
like soap in water. Dare to realize, and
weld forging of two, ask—get soapy

life mere twist into synecdoche, how you
stand for that. Into the position set
go there you go beautifully racing

flap of skin, hairdryer—the picking foam
set you go sadly beneath din stars
7.4% of the vote in London bang

nature into action potentials I don't see
how the alright. What a string of crap.
What a pang. To create, lather mix in

busted leg cloud not that. You dust
off the mimic, dust away my eyes.
An inner tradition of this exceeds panic.

4.

Some cops boo. Evidently run about pin
airbag down make a ripped off picket
stunned. If you want to change the

tick alright. Everyone's so—lymphatic
drainage from a primary lust for, tends
to, agrees with, makes a stab at

wouldn't if you, swigs sickeningly that
drained call it a gab. Against the
lust to scrape you out set up objections

in a grid, circled with flowers. Some
them are gay. Imagine if you
did an orgasm every once you have to

accept at—sneezes away news, my
back is demotic, my front also is demotic,
leg is, penis is. I am not democratic.

5.

Sing with the wind that bashes across asphalt
round her house with trees leaking
my bent eyes scattering salt over,

except that the—at first, I thought you
were crazy all that life, frittering
back happiness to offset

in the guise of compulsion, happiness itself.
You leg it. You cloud over.
Our government does not care about spitting

justice from the awash grin a shot
planned through the dark. What you do
in lights is a sort of shadow-preening

one tomorrow picket that it's used up
two soap polyglactin cloud cops
steel alright. If I can just that adapt.

ITER E SANGUINE

Survive life likely to remain intact for
only the craziest splits was he finically
contorted does she start wanting the
tag it comes with. Necessary scraps of
it drift, are naturalized in the big
idea of oblivion feed, a life wanted
to a pure fault that won't be nullified.

Something she had and tore out. How did
you do it, waiting for the distribution
of cars to thin, lights of a more certain
damage to rush slowly along the elected freeway,
set to convert its freight into
anticlimax? What make? Your own in
the kind of elapsed thrall too

much definitely vague. Stories come and
I ghostwrite stupid across their patina go
mad indifferently wait. Smack at
next the elasticated nonuple glazing
drift, incredibly into a lane placed on
stilts kicking piss off. He assembles into
her shouting. Their love was impossible

to deny even and insidiously blatant
me along. Separate: of real-world single-vehicle
too crashes, once the slides off
control of that swapped for being dead
end it. Real lights come from real
people shifted by are the means of
this to contort you to a corpse. I want you

not desperately yet to die thrown scratch over
that bent road to embed yourself in
twisted erotic, sheet glass disassembled
on that patch you last out briefly.
Want me back this way. The infinite
stick crabbiness that love dissolves as
time flips wraps suddenly that head she

or I was remember, I make up shit like
impossibility singularized, made compact
fixed on, in a moment about
to get sung beautifully across the speeding
agony of traffic in a voice to destroy
the life it is, the rational hysteria of that
life and all its business trashed out,

flicked into nothing. What does news
report number whatever think of that
it thinks, when strangely I was a child I
fought every night to wake up my
love just the simplest conversation would
do I needed you that easily and often
smashed vodka on the patio. Took my

hands in my own life to mean something
withheld permanently. There was no point in
waiting for you because I couldn't
fail to do that, dictating the order of pain
you ought to suffer e.g. first switch that
tv off now throw water over your smoking
face please, wake up. The shattered

glass like a salt sea-wave, dot after dot on
your life away. Nothing assigns itself
to the crash-stop patented as ultimate detox
and waits. You actually did wait for the lights to
rush close and consuming all hesitancy
then and the precise brilliance of it, the
exactness of that consumption of obsolete

smack into. Then what do you make of
it later such acquiescence as the net amp
start of the world. In a parallel lyric they are
still flashing, gradually at the white-striped
and soft edge of the decision to live,
gently not taken. I take it. That reality in
effect is a speciality, get seen through

caustic glaze of, shattering begins that
no provision of love would end. Spinning
the circle of Apollo softly round
its defrost cycle the dial warped in fire and dribbling
on a haircut finished with. And once
the consumption matches the wait you
imagine with a split open heart she's dead.

FOR LIFE

How must pressure withstand me I damp
occlude it. Because deposited things
the verbs fly about and stash food everywhere
rushes to meet her at the street clap
together lit fists. As if in a dream balanced on
aghast the thin exited air I tilt, my
neck erect, biscuits and eye-stubs bobbing over
a long day started in reeds by the dark

green knit-together scar patches throw,
creates area for more future in your life too
want to sit next. When I look at your
face sorted into reasons glowing beneath
sun bag that before incredibly I lose
you forever. Kick a fly's teeth out, valid in
scrap leapt incorrigible to remain your
lover stitched open beady-face. Can't go

on just remaining. If I need you
in this skin thistle-ended and trapping me,
again to be sunk right through my body,
all the crack concessions fit. Run
away from my inflatable glue-box tin
ear cleared up table is an arranged spirit
hoovering the sky. Now rain surreptitiously
originates in your mouth, clamped there.

LIFE INCREASER

for Jeremy Hardingham

1.

Pushing my face tight up exquisite into
the neat glass, impressing
can you again star in her throat,
as a flung-out undiscountable and alive
question of your
                            sincerity at last could
            alone crack apart the tin lid on
            something I threw together, she
                                        is different now
scarpering amid this visible set of
wrecks and pins up a breeze to
carry away news of who
            for you massacre the glass snot-eyed,
                        I am prepared first
                        last to grin, has
                        again to whip up a point
thickening out, to a new life in discharged
sight of the worst candy sliced off
            sort of managerial or technocratic nar
            few elementary remarks neces
            as it is sometimes employed, "elite"
            scene of a green plat, cream of
                        morning Helicon,
            it does nothing to resist my
            teeth also splitting off a limp glass-shred,
whistling through faked
                            ice again and anyone

except you would love
        I need in havoc that righted love
        will spit unless myself out
late we stopped in the road continued to kiss
wouldn't stop you
had to leave dissociating me for instant
thrills from life which, left
                        completely and
        to chance that
        is to say everything itself can
        be here only,
                in principle eat out the whole airport.

2.

Dear angel of impeccable dispirit, aghast at your
beauty flimsiness and scant being-for-sex,
I cry at the wind shrunk by
                        you waspishly pan to
        tongue on tongue, grit
        filmic scintillating my old leg's dashboard,
        paste over the
picture of a bill a picture of your face equated,
                in the hot springs
        northern South Africa, women street
sellers providing glue
my angel you bit my neck, I ran my hand over
your ass molten
                        rushes in my raw cock sat
down and discussed this
        only applied to the modern world
        follows that Lenin couldn't

again it's a question of "job consciousness"
picnic drill
                    at which the
replaced glass is a wince in
planar and elaborated by much duct-taped
pushes my tongue through
                    should I take on you angel,
                    lost to the
battery-heart findings of acute insight, sung apart
also clinched, also swatted,
                              canvassing against
the lie of a smashed-away sheet-planet, my
opinions
                    e.g. France
                    hardly "backward"
                    any conventional econ. index
                    eat as much as you
can you wring that face angelically and bust,
force of dispirit, good pride and joy,
          returning to the filth of life scandalously pin
          me again into it, my
          sweet angel drooping and sweaty, cock
                    first or at
          least immaculately,
                    completely destroy their luck tilt.

3.

The safe-house was manacled by rock on
either side shifting to a heap slowly
enough that we could see, Jeremy when you and
I walked there

how are you now
stuck bagging affections in a blank hurry for lust,
nothing less
than everything etc.

                    and love, got a clasp to
                    quicken it
          die for
                    Czechoslovakia, crisps, smoke
          drips forward icily
          no estranging
what does it mean that I balance my life
on belief that a consummate pressure to
live within me can't
          let up, scores a few points by
          dished-out
          walk screaming to the launderette
floppy, sense-continence
          burning to let go and grin, stacked behind the
          beat glass worrying itself,
glass polished with a ripped tongue to reclusive syrup,
                    pushing through
you situate
                    rain flushing in a tied-up descent no
          sex out but life brought
out this time just incredibly, just
and screwed to bits, faster than a speeding bandage
          stripped tentatively from
          to the blown-up face of this exquisite ant's
nest hoovered bingo
                              gap-gummed
          streak of the saw across Palestine, which you
          are in secret, sole-deep

thrashing through the spray of salivated tin into
        messes of glass to
            at last in my self-failing arms be all wished for,
                        all the true
            and impossible, fact-stopped
            ruin of decreasing life, aghast
spectrally in the U.S.A. embassy canteen shit-faced
                and still singing, takes
                    up her beautiful mouth and walks out.

NEUTRALITY
2004

More than anything it is freedom that I hate
O banality of its disimpaction be remembered
let its indigestible shit-phalanx be on vacation
life insinuated in wicker ice and back-ordered is
by this lovely psychosis more kept up again.

The poll apt to be most rightly reflective
of freedom is incarcerated in the bloodstream
its periodic melos shit administrates, clean out
however of what written in shit itself is
called political significance that blood stutters.

And what is shit, whose own not unusual
disimpaction can ameliorate the posture of him
crouching with his eyes shut, as my love cannot
so shake a blood clot that it reliquefies it
is the perfect regularity of loss traded for need.

Hatred of freedom is not a consequence
of shit per se buttered up to disclose the flip
secrets of its world even to the screaming
baby now dispersed through the cerebellum in sweet
bullet points but is allowed differently.

If you drive three miles the hatred will in
the same time drive seven, likewise in front
of the teeth shit decommissions when my
lips are apart the rupture they propagandize
can fade in its thus futile comparison with hatred.

If this square represents the via negativa
and inside this square there is incarcerated a circle
pinned so it affronts no barrier of the square but
floats in my milky blur of fructose and galactose,
this disbelieved is the unending circulation in love.

SAFE BET

Pious belief in nothing flips on, in the
wing flipping about where the goosed
life feeder blinks. Intractably ice keeps for
months in a red sponge cut to
addresses torn out, cheekbones slid
and slept away this
                              is nothing going it
                              has a route you
are it now. Does substitute word here
do this substitute word for when, crying along to
make a point do what. The chiliasm
defrosted by a yawn spitting around it is it
wet-wipes in an overheated chip pan
belief in nothing it is the golden ring element
                              say I
                              do that
is say nothing but shop around for less I
do that. Look up from the street, to the
pole, then slowly to the metal square with
kill your speed on it. Later on we
the cab is here, the procession is waiting
for its floor trips on salt clutches
                              at its ice brainrail
                              no-one to eat
the wet-wipes even raw, in the ballot
substitute box-word gargling vomit in
time with the carotid pulsation of a hand over
mouth sovereignty. Belief in every
oat duct of the core devaluation of nothing
else but that flames unending away,
                              going to die
                              dying to go

reds better run. Take the wing off with its
joke of a ligament and stuff it in the disposal unit.
To be convinced about the route without
foaming all over the till try: I can't take it any
more or less a bubble in insecticide and
am not asked to. I move to the floor
                    that's now
                    here I can't
take care it anywhere going to panic. Then
I lose. Then with a stapler flick upon
the cloud a jet. At the hospital they put me
under on morphine on top of cocaine
I wanted nothing I spent the
six months after that attempting
                    not to stop
                    being almost dead
and nothing is easier. But with that
option come duties ranked like the squint
and gaze at a nominal cut, to come
up slap against air sick-dressed and drowning
breath out be the infibulated citharœdic
roll-call to democracy a stuck fast
                    forward
                    button bang in its hole.

MOTHER SHORNEY

What became of the anti-war coadunation walked
her tricycle through a square. There was this
mat before the diocese of thirst and piss
we advanced up to it, with our face we talked
the small change in and the metal shelf moves
back and then forth and cleans it out.
               Disagreeable ovoid
               bacterium chiefly nonmotile wet as
               fuck who licked

remit these brine flies. USFA what you need
to know. Are the accidents that have nothing to
do with my life whatever I want. Through
a window the agreement crested in shit-bleed
the small change in and the metal shelf moves
back and then forth and cleans it out.
               And ground truth
               data show the pier
               osculates the horizon.

The shooting deaths at Camp Ganci. Afterward
we advanced up to it, that have nothing do
without my life, over through a square you
know something about. Endurance is assured
with oil torture in and the metal shelf moves
back and then forth and cleans it out.
               You drink too much
               I love you
               strangely, in spite of it.

AP OB NUAT

Stunned gut shifts in a mimicry of distracted
is it lived, ready for my having, done to
sit will it depute scars, finical outlast reel
the sea in flippant to your gapped
and shut up routine tantamount to dioxane
remember that dream where the shop or
                         it the beginning of a
                         shop climbed up
their stairs burnt scattered idem aminobutyric
to tell me when to call a professional and
eat its face. Undue our that shaped Ogia
Redline Kavinga Golf Bag body throws up
its all its hands scripted to peel, feet rationed
out to the grout mat like duffel. Keen
                         to know you
                         too get triply below-scored
your three lines of whipped teeth chattering
your flood-door plaque inmost, fall out
bus window on a joke because each customer applic
unique opening nominal 4' x 8', hinged,
deputed, blood skipping around the dryer,
whose heart is a motto polished too stupid
                         dyed sherbet-rot,
                         elicit grief for it
dyed red. For people wishing more and
their glyph wiped clean in its cortical washout
make true noise, sex prediction abrupt. Be
so negative the lights fizz and go out restoring
a possessed black dazzle, to which spongy adamant
conundra whipped up and shining. Pindar
                         grease in its sandpit
                         log insert do

up that mimicry, is what you did dioxane on
the door latch pecker asks really this or
that dream where and the lobby and is
it too lived too much you are next anodising
cannot, is dead. Wolves prowl at the bar,
milk on their dread escutcheon, recurring
                              nightly like a living
                              pimp to its chlorinated sinus.

Evidence suggests that in the male guinea pig
you've got plastic tits. Merely to harden the
blow not otherwise roughly squatted to, but in
they do peel off, any case of Muslim litter
heads cum vaginas trees etc. Corticosteroidal
punctuation id rips thus into buzz syntax, all for
                              you taking off
                              O common periplaneta
americana lipid, capital winged with awe
and shock to its hard bargain basement into
the foxholes dug in my face. The metaphors
link up to enrich their bearer, a pearl
necklace jokingly dubbed tax exempt. There
they go, votes thrown up in the brightening
                              new sky to tinkling
                              accompaniment played
out magisterial on the rococo guilt celeste it
is the music of our publicised spheres and their good
looking new haircuts. Dissidence in this
way is banalised without the end it couldn't

possibly need anyhow. Bitch for your lives.
What is the antonym of lettuce. Ralph Nader
                        eating a catsuit dip
                        file out the syrupy fire
door broken beneath snow. In the albino rat's
liver sex percolates too you have to be it
for free your mind urges like a bus receipt,
gut stunned, ileum knot flamboyant thymic
cracker in the gill. Romance. It cannot as you
now breathe and then do a habit make time
                        work then be a lot
                        more easily more or
less dead. We follow the pimp to the bracket,
situate in the Creda belt poly vee its dysphagic
replica of a creamed itch, making sure nothing
but you is tried; to follow that in beautiful
lilies of blood retrojected across the ozone in
love history sanitise its window with dioxane,
                        a little more or less
                        today or else tomorrow.

Panic alive rota bidden hostile for it. Gargled
hype serum spat about. Make the tinned
up greased tractable lust fold, act balanced
but fail skids, advances and rips into a pithy
new being matched to the limit of need
and care so blind with erotic belonging that
                        is my pâté get
                        CRE 12 be discount

it that eager. Dark neoprene spritz at the utmost
heat belted to a hyperemic desert to mat nothing in
your hair is a waste of time. Walk with me
into the garden. There is a project there we
lovers stare away its root. In the swerving
desire cast as a gross net gain finical sideline
                              keloid, stretched in
                              the pull of polemic to
a complete new body-wrap tailored to bleed straight
into the budget venting hose. With a rose
blush on. The money you earn making that
the hold in you defining how caresses sit with it
the picture of that money on the grit rink all
these all of them at myriad sample innards
                              is pitched VA 26
                              wednesday again
go on your nerve. There is a rejected titanium bolt
fit your cheek on remember that, in the stucco
at neck-height, there is its hydrophobic and yellow
bracket shone up by a rash of laughing sellotape,
what you be yourself. Drinking the bound water
to death backlit through a gut less runny out
                              of the breath for it
                              dryer, in a surplus
this ecstatically underestimated, this sheraton exit
bled before end. Day after day augment
superannuation scheme pursuant to paragraph 4
or 90 scratched into the toilet seat next to
an advertisement for your imaginary cock in
the dream they skitter twist and warp but
                              are mimicry is a flame
                              suppression trioxane tit pinger.

SONG OF THE WANKING IRAQI

Bust those sluts anal thrashing to imagine
in a room with no windows or doors with
a metal pipe along the wall a ferro-concrete
roof nobody inside and a vapour fed in
through the pipe in short jets the temperature
is right so the vapour won't evaporate it
can be permethrin hated by crayfish with each
jet the room is more full very slowly
it will fill and the vapour become a total block
of liquid which the room sheathes and the
room is categorically a void no-one is in it
had the floors tiled sills cleaned and repaired
and toilets showers and a new medical
center added Renoir did a picture he called a
girl with a watering can we look at the world
from her own altitude in the national
gallery of art washington 39 ½ × 28 ¾ in
we left off with the vapour turned into
a block but suppose we now change the heat
of the room nobody inside innocent
teen in first throating would it be better
from a conceptual art perspective to turn it
up or down ask General Karpinski
the conditions inside are better than at home
that you won a no obligation savings
diploma in biodynamic psychotherapy it is
enjoined to meet with an inner heart
to clash and collide and throw its spark
slowly into the room there is no room
for it the army is the tongue you stick out
the lips round it are pork crackling bent up
the street you circle like nobody there

are these ways to imagine they put on a
good show we could hardly have done it
better ourselves the chemical light is
snapped the phosphoric liquid is dropped
to the lees into him but he prefers the
broom handle it can go all night like
capital itself in the grip of the cupidity
of the 372nd Military Police Company.

ODE TO SQUID

Go down stand up a desiccant in skin pack
descend avid cutis aflame track nil will
discounting you tack along it sag for
better dew-eating moon on the bed garbage
are ways to is them worse or strip its
wanted the best sex nothing but nothing
                            but butter lungs
                            fascinated it inside
a shop crossfire from the interestingly divided
benches beyond you and must continue
hold up national feature of exists rain in door
track one end track million go put on
the mind which this one which that one that
was that ticks my hand slapped out inner
                            appetite in brasso
                            you direct a new film
the film is about a squid uprising in the rings
of aspirin-shaded winter light around
Bangkok and salad and a freak number plate
renin by the thorax-load is a fountain in it
counterinsurgency is to be its foam escarpment
as upon it rains a stiff brew of wet liquefied
                            and mixed up kids
                            the deputy chief
staff may shout let there be civic action a model
for the operations of your film to follow in
these colours yellow for the aspirin shades red
black or nothing for the calamari indigo is
out for the general staff who get a bel canto
cameo and choke on liquefied and immiscible sex toys
                            given my heart
                            you not

do it a shit turn but to preserve it you took it
I worked for you not to be kicked out
but for reward to get back I was content
to do it but not to be paid as in the event it happened
one bench or two track forty billion go on
on but since there is nothing inside you
                              appetite in cif that
                              is reasonable to
bawl and be indifferent wastes my time and I
give up the chief of staff for operations in
bright wonderful shadows of serotonin hack up
acidic dew over the cartons of squid sauce
you are not alone in wanting to make love for him
unsatisfied with woe and unsatisfied also
                              with your desire
                              but insured by art
against the failure to excuse yourself but it is
enjoyable to make up death when death
is the death of need feign some default eat more
people out to decapitate the deputy fax
orange hole-punch gray cocks tumbling out or
around the dry mouth of a retro conarc in the
                              cubicle appetite in
                              a bleach shines
steadfast its starry pinprick because the bleach is
black no leaping up or diving say goodbye and
come back please come back departing
from the fire which a wick of ice chokes up bitten
off he who believes his fist will bear this
truth into the shattered noon air rips out
                              plugs of water
                              he snorts up the sandpit.

THE CREDIT SHOT

Serial killer Oreo cookie stacking competition plug
    climax the extras are extra can't work won't
not in this lunch again a word out of you
    top down brain to genitals gut to flush out bag

experience the wind, flare in its perennial end easy
    do that the gap from pâté the magnificent
seat of divination to its nacho upholstery neuter it
    eat the prophetic throat serial killer Oreo

differ no gap only a lay-by in the wind there is wet
    information the brain dries it experience
her funnel she is a game news on the ASX tilting
    competition plug and its frothing yellow ash

see to it that reality needs you screw in it swallow
    it whole bag it Folkets Dagblad Politiken
bandit elements Anarkhia not imprudent or all eaten
    not fear difficulties or pinpricks chicanery

insults and persecution from the liquid tableau
    killer Oreo instead flare up it is not easy
and the support of the masses increase to members
    sex lieutenants of the capitalist class plug

is crystal clear what follows you from bed to
    sink in your hands do it climax dryly on here in
frothing yellow air tucked into its serrated arc
    is your infantile disorder stacking competition.

HÉROÏDE PASTEL

Coerce the virgin plastic grains it snorts up,
      to scales matched by
it won't ripped like competitors', a tee
      blindfold in crunchy iron—
scurrilous to enamour my walk to
      that parse tree, that you live
off way lined exactly up for a spray
      bullet-points on olive—
in the national gallery of art, Washington
      the statue by Barthelémy Prieur
is 181.5 × 64.3 × 49.2cm, weeps its
      surfactant into a diaper—
it peels away brick-colour, trees that ice
      soil or metal in the busy
flesh are one, with ready doxa laminates,
      pulp to a staggering lonely head.

Erotic grist pinches against its chalk barrier
      wrapping my brain,
you smacked carpet of pâté idea squat tight,
      and the idea is bright—
dishy as fuck, shape of a wing-mirror buried
      in deeply in a slick of
vomited fingernails, mouth which a chunk
      of piss seals—
I can't see any more help they have the
      most amazing doggy bags
except canned, on to its ideal balance-sheet
      scribbled is the plea—
bayonet, uphill back the reflection given
      to my life origin
panto crater keep out of direct
      darkness or drip like fire away.

On the rear of the spine a stencil-drawing
        of an elated baby
wish-list on the scissors themselves is
        is scrawled, be right—
pushes this face off, at rededicate a cinch
        play through the clouded
won't rip it savagely but all civil like glass
        replenished stab-hole—
bits of life crumble from spit on
        screens, licensed
so incendiary what their dispatch thrills
        right to fake ice—
but the sound mirrors the surplus, annuls
        what it's detached
from O Sancta Justitia Bass/Pf racket
        trumpetful of cum.

DILDO ODE

Eat them a snow roast the atmolysis dead
pretty a new way. They had tied me
on a stool fully clothed out the window but
in the episode and reached my head.
Sex shone in them flush mounted dirt-bag
lingam with the yoni, who fed the
its drip through retard sic you
                         take love in at
                         three speeds e.
g. cop / hen. Inside them is a comb for
saliva who don't want in that. So quick
they are likely to love you. But too
far inside hooded in pin suds. They sound
they swap eating they clot about jog
sounds like glycosuria, inside the sugar
free speech enclosure dap choking
                         up on worked
                         up
hot vaseline spit you up for pith their toothless
toy ileum squeaks when you bounce it
you do not bounce it you become a hole
sensitive and nervous the pleasure of sharing
talk in the spray-proof hutch. For the
cavalcade dries through its wind and will
is possible like a moistened planet that
                         is wet
                         indirect debit set
and go. Come yourself. They are the foundation
of the book others are allegorical.
They watched, some of them smoked.

Then let her arms hang at her sides put
their stool in, in whose hearts is admitted their
perversity follow the part thereof that
is there to die against, is again deep
                                    up them
                                    imperial tobacco.

Hesitate to contact us. You come with a lock
at the front of the belt and dream them
are not it. The Democratic convention gild
own throat ender kit they retroflect on acid in
their melody you all get some. From the
honey where the bat drowned scoop out
of wirecutters, let them drop into a bowl of hot
                                    otex minus
                                    a hole
you are in the hole. Tonight we have with us
NTE5 note position white / orange. If this
square sits within another, and its pins are set
apart at intervals measured by our circle
try this: truth is eternal and or dead and is
the movement flattered by static to
living fused in three, the fierce transparent sky
                                    is its perpetual riot,
                                    our trap with no admission.
No shit is good shit. On a bracket are
audible countersunk pozi-cross head zinc so on.
You can get attached and always get
out if they do, forcing an oyster at gunpoint to

fuck sawdust for payout in nuance. They ranged
themselves about the room, resting on the
edges of its couch leaning in half-meant
                              and relax
                         at speed one
nonchalance against the walls, papered
with fiery orchids, watched her remove my
car and go down in smoke. Safety
matches negation. Should they want you to
be more can punish your leg in stab it rend
hair vend erotogenesis push up to that glass
crackling in an art deco of eyelashes,
                              know where
                         you are with that.

Once went by licensed spontaneity roused
away crowds smashing windows in the name
of freedom with the prettiest emptiness.
Hire them by the broker's dozen, a livid trail
noughts into the telesphere. But with the
rise of organised working class movements
spontaneity itself shifts, the name burns
                         a hole
                    full of suspirable
blood into its gelid tag crazed off their
foot of the bed. Speed two, fingers in the wet
cookie lobe crossed like a street by fire
trucks conjuring a desire for what is dead
if necessary impossibility is dead. That is

a name for truth excess wire. The standpoint
of limbs in a flood of hate for their
                        own your life
                        tag in
raptorial total orgasm and living riotous joy
at kicking the faked edge of a life in
commodity-sepia to hell and knowing it
is a dream only in the crassest last fantasies.
Only the most fatuous and deep-down catatonic
vote casters stifle paranoia, they keep
their fridge stocked with a thousand reflective
                        slips of
                        ice and gaze as
if not dead then wait. They are likely to love
you comb. Plan to need less eaten
shit and more of none of it. In the sky over
my throat which is still fierce transparent
as the riot of truth, like an attack in some
joke war a joke storm of sleet thrashes down
it is fragments of the newly annulled
                        dildo you are
                        invited to eat them.

ROHYPNOL

You scrapped back to life irrigate
    it perforated funnel here does that
itself its spout burn its apart inward
    child screaming its teeth up its
ass on a remote control resin hod
    an ease with which they can be poured

want to own your life no why own
    it it there goes its specific shift on
crack pulpotomy amend my dead
    and beginning future where the
stones and rivers and trees against
    sunk-out glass tilt in ineffectively

one hundred or one billion quid
    to ashes for librettos its afters for
screamed ice ecstatically claws at
    the things we do against loved
dinner for carrot it is irreplaceable
    quakes to be finished up early

good enough in this account sales office
    I walk to the cabinet and from
to the till only for invoices next
    which an invoice continuation pad
is there and mud on the window outside
    which to love you must first vomit.

LIVERY

That there is the humidity, that dumb licking
bacterium forked up is blood, is your own.
It cinches into that outline, is federal and day after
one day in a puce towel rots go blowfish crimper
crazy mated interred up and devastated by a
passion in its stages for that lip there is
                              this for you off-white
                              hot perfume bolted on
that calx gone soft, be famished for a touch that
perfect that analysed spite go snaps into
and act the descent of flesh livid uninterested
light scraped out from the puddle of darkness
to the shore where the shore massaged is about
that close to this lip outline. Throw in
                              your head to chew
                              it look xanthomonas be
it upset in the back garden make a way to
be that live with it, hot decay as the noise of losing
softens under this skin it infundibulum cap burnt
eyes in a crisp bag, in this fountain. Do you want
take this back, reel in an outline of what that is that
is left to die for next which trait which it is this
                              colour of yellow
                              them scraped out
picket in easy money burnt off, pick burning
now with a desire. At the right decency of flesh, cut
and repaired such a risible phoenix also then going
along with love, in one part chlorox nine
parts water running too late to wait thickened in
better again to catch it out the fire puts itself last
                              you know this
                              is the drill, drink up.

The highs don't last but neither does withdrawal
race into their place, your life does. Shit does
this abstract sift love into its acne scars you roll down
a window that there is your body take a reason
to live as it as this for granted, to stand as its blood in a grid
and shake your ass. But what is creosote
                        not for if you
                        that rocky descent to
bright tryptophan in piss, that fluctuations in the rate of
profit stimulate a crisis observable forever through
the pink glass of its display closet you lick you
stick it's that freezing but this ice now adequates to
the transmitter in correct mind damage. Blow this
torch out this hoover. In its outline, scrambling
                        begging away
                        its whole pivot to slap
bang in the relocated edge clutching to resort
that way to me, this sensation of an unintelligible
halt cannot getting your call in from a base
of a cone cannot wait on you the brushes in a tree
that that humidity screens out, waking
and taking turns its solitary gang-bang
                                repositioned across it that
                                car slide
slide it on dead, rip a line out. The highs do
last the noise of losing dies away, this is your
own new blood take it. Ritornello yellow
and scraped, a shoplight withers over the syringe
and the air is anaclitic and the stars seen through
it dab it against this sciatica, and finally against
                        the wrong eye burning
                        like a ring of benzene.

So what do you just drink yourself to death
just tired working hard appreciated however as
a runnel can death really be said to get any nearer
spits you in the vocoder, on the granulated march
fistule KBR extinction contract panicking to
too many clouds, too much queasy marine life
                              check this faucet rpm
                              nail the plastic bowls down
later to fold them up. You are a good helping and
you are told that in outline. Nearly enough
love today but the resentment of passion wasn't there
then was passion there is this it can you fold me
that up melatonin syringed into a more risible eel at
is scattering my flame fatuously, its dots on
                              top its leaves scar
                              take shit out for a meal
Parsons Corp. A deeper cracking and scraping noise
it is raining prawns are here now the right seat is up
take me to a night in the world, to get that lately free
of need look. It is indubitable that the Arabs want
gameshows just as in the foyer you said to me
that you wanted sexual happiness for the animals
                              stripped and lined up
                              in their diversity
constituting for us both a discouraging frieze of fur
but you did not say that they would get it
so will they get it. Forced conical stint palpation or
not you are what you are, try what you like
for nothing. In conclusion the pâté windowcleaner
door latch spring shit ice and water to be seen
                              with are these.
                              They'll get you in anywhere.

NEOCOSIS
2005

Neither death nor crime exists in the polymorphous world of the burlesque where everybody gives and receives blows at will, where cream cakes fly and where, in the midst of the general laughter, buildings fall down. In this world of pure gesticularity, which is also the world of cartoons (a substitute for lost slapstick), the protagonists are generally immortal ... violence is universal and without consequences, there is no guilt.

Pascal Bonitzer, *Le Champ aveugle* (1982)

FALLING IN LOVE CREAM CRAB

Now itch like precision flamecutting. Detected
sweat in bloom Pakistani Sukhoi-30MKI,
sweat that eyes in the front of your head crunch,
pulse on detergent, broken ear on Anantnag
bus ride flowering to a throat full of sweat,
brighter than the consumption reel it cap fades for
                              no-one half
                    se
by half second and is nothing except love there
is nothing except it on. Back flowing fade
you point a skeleton at, sweat on it
on it is the wool/teeth foreclosures ½ off skeleton,
the no-one your flesh is slung on burning its
with desire FTIR spectr. In China the
                              ©
                    Let Us Put You
touch into dead green: hit aflame by
lips switched cutting the dead air dead volts
scattered by holding your face on dying
palms in the thrill of a kiss you cry for –
a bat drops. Planets drop in. A bat
stopgap for the IAF. Make more by working
                              cry for –
                    less
life TBA by my shred hands wringing the bridge by
Dartford into • *clavicle sorbet,* • new *tibia bake,*
new *uln* / under you grabbing your face act
calm orgasming frantically in you needing you
would the person whose car is parked
to esteem the pram full of scissors in Morgan Stanley,
                              Houston,
                    Taipei,

Now expand into the Netherlands. Into the
line booster fade you point a skeleton at
it is the skeleton imagined dead; its mirroring in
your faced life not at a time forever not for
anything scratched in patty where the reverse is
true to mere form, dying. Get out
                              bed
                              of
• new *Lumbar Vertebrae Ranch Squid,* | nail – skip to •
Preparation Tips in Frum Mix, set shaking
unfree of its off switch, broken on the heart pro
rata cut while you wait. You make dinner with
Nancy Zucker Boswell from Transparency International
look stupid. You sheathe the IAF in ice,
                              faster
                              than
reason is your immediacy. Wait and see
it. It is nothing except love, its cast of paroxysms gets
the dead air plastered, abiding in Asset Liability
Management • new 1 John 3.17 *ia bak* McNamara
to Wolfowitz his brother in need and closes
negotiations on the master derivatives Sunny Delight
                              Kids Cove
                              lockout and riot
leatherette integument for the bat. It drops
are on hold. You have been placed in a queue
on hold. You have been placed in a queue are
Verkehr in the community, substitute to produce alternative

puns with *fakir*, with *quaere*, and finally
with *hair*, i.e., hair in the community, in its throat sweat,
                      free fish
                      oil for kids

Now get nowhere fast. Anantnag running on
the pram full of hedging needs in Ann Veneman X
paroxysmic you arise, just now sincerely
Chinese for the first time, locking your car.
The temperature is at 3480. We deliver.
Love is the angle of the mirroring it breaks for,
                      the pivot
                      are bet
you on track for. Nothing but love in the face that
aflame steel discolours red. You remember
kissing my mouth, traducing the oxyacetylene
whisper cut out. Later in the ear I
again am in an encounter with the skeleton you
point at going. There are feet everywhere
                      you tread
                      on
them cap with your 1.6 way mirror • new *tarsals*, • •
1. credit aspect 7, plastic 8 way meet clients'
hold you – throttle out sex in Palam debt product,
your eyes a must-see, icing as they flower in
beauty vanilla bonds • n. What this means is that
placed in a face they flash out incomparably
                      wild back
                      flowing fade

and I love you really there is nothing but love over
it is all there is there nothing other
than it no there by where the cylinders are fitted
patella bol with regulators and flexible hoses which lead
to the blowpipe. It will make your mouth water
freeze, a life aflame in the shark shit,

                              only now forever,
                              1.9

ROGER AILES

Our money is where your mouth is, clammy as that
strict blip of successive exit holes, into the light over
which is dubbed the light in filth-blistered orthognathic 2D flying
elf neon crossbar 261. To buy it if you see
what we mean is to see by it: nothing matters more
any time, just kick back / any time, in moccasins
in a group of business men who deal on Art export it
you just skip back three lines now
than being in the dark (in maybe better than out).
Among several adjustments coming up is the adjustment
of the mood lighting. And action. Adjust the mood
lighting with our view to a good enough good
match made in:

> The *real* peritoneum of Aristotle.
> The bedroom.
> The western planet.
> The *real* peritoneum of Socrates.
> Ohio.
> The system.

tch made in: Diebold-owned basinasal SEXX shout out
your name here: Kia-Ora. There is some spunk on
the nail clippers in your mobile phone Irving you dickhead.
It's for the thinking man's population,
you pull the flush and BP petroleum like a cyclone fills
all the contented air from the wax ring to the bolt caps.
The characters will be Sergio et al. It will be
hard to read but strange, sounds like:

> *every striation laps pat to it*
> *and flickers silk latin salad flourish.*
>> (Prynne, *Poems* 438)

And the blue in the face will glow like the sky
light of fat-free ice, all alone you're up for the phased exit
from Hull manufacturing. To run out of a mind
to speak not just for standing in

                        as a foam bun, it is
                        what it is
                        passion the agon
again in its occasionally antic and yet serious too
milk substitute for polymerizing my lid. It is what
it is and what is it it bleeds you dry for, on nights on
days on any shift in the universe

                            of stars

                            vault now puce
in fact on the verisimilitudinous rim shift itself, I
know there is tinned – am tinned I get up
and I go am asked, I get up by you irrit. fibroma what
is Roger Ailes and where. I call you at three in
him but not in the CEO part only the unspoiled penis,
I get down to the unspoiled protoplasm of his eros,
down to where it is dark and there are no sounds
Shah of the anti-banana republica, maybe sublated
into his icteric salute to Allah coming
up next. If he is him then who am I, and
who are you in the coconut shy – but you are Sergio
was it you said. And then again if he isn't, if no
such thing in fact *is*, then watch it because is
that you that flip-chart, then. The ass of this end is helical
/ screwed-down and probably not easy to tilt,
Sergio, 500 affiliates by the middle of next anything
you roll yourself into a tube we can make it
into your life for the taking – yes later but fuck all that
                        (repeated later)

instead you shit meringue in a choke hold: Fox
is arrive now have we obtain the future our folk are real
need it you bet it did – new coverage new
exit hole in the throat to slip and pant through. Who will
                yet slip 8
                cents to 3
                3.07
                and still be happy
                submits that what we
need is irony, a kind maybe of periphrasis, e.g. one
of those riddling and ceremonious subordinate
clauses faking nostalgia for pastoral, the words in it
                could be *bent reed, on fire, Pot Rice,*
or, materialistically
                a diisocyanate is reacted with a diol
                a word with you
sit spitroasted eclectically by 17.16 and 39.74 both,
thinking, they should be metaphors for the limits of compassion
and of its downturn, a kind of melancholy
or equally metaphors as breasts, Nesquik shot up a scalene eyeball
a medium of getting what face got the shit on 5
                O vision
scabbard rot before you break and are too late: unmade yet
already never dying they
                alone fly are a peristaltikos my
life shudders under their unfinishable tearing
you can't eat it you get it for nothing
                search/news?fr=news
                something about *a significant player*
                The way of Athens.
                no another O,

all in a tube. But, fuck all that. Set on fire the anti-mirror,
the headlights on the car going steady in front,
with Furtwängler doing Bach on the/my front speakers,
sex five-minute top-of-the hour the price of victory
is right read the hole in the water at the top you
made in Taiwan by breathing. It is nothing yet once
in you it shimmers like the cracked open sea,
within and without my eyes, in my open breathing
heart tanned pink. Does it recapitulate ap/ap_en_
stuff me to the hilt stuff or values a shade more excellent
rashes, allergies, Borax, alum, free washing soda,
Borax is the odd one out for the taxidermist
– from here you can get out by satirising disorientation
yes the flirting with getting out can be negative and not a *forte*
yes the disorientation is not political when it comes to it.
It is a disorientation of language. The nostalgia
           for pastoral stretches freely to material
           and signifier, rhymed with week-day.
           The anguish of that.
           The *angoisse* (Mallarmé).
You will never be the same again after your hair is going.
Alternatively by 29.96 – 47.76; *alternatively*, mind – .
Each way you look at it the trap it the low end of 52-week
frantic to be more loved. You been here a long
time Sergio if you feel like taking a leak or doing something
else like it on me. Without needing to be asked
twice I took the lift, stabbing the button for the thirteenth
floor and we both grinned all the way up: the news
was bad from the East, Zarobad gustatory in his crypt;
but good from the West: more rolling blackouts.

Therefore, SAN ANTONIO – a diisocyanate is gill
ant player if not then Clear Channel Communications
Inc. the my most popular station operator my most
radio station operator, has picked Fox News Radio
to be the primary source of national news for most
of its news and talk stations, officials announced Monday.
I don't know how to be who you want me to be,
but anyway am worth dying for it, look front with your total blood,
a significant worker. Instructions: A paper rectangle with
the following dimensions plays the orgasm your body
has at the photocopier, sort of thinking of Albert
Wohlstetter and his influential advocacy of precision.
Then an event,
A wet cry in the black night, sponges whip up the air,
toluene my officials my announced mine it.

       But, fuck all that.
       Undesired
(1) isomers lob up walnuts rearward of the cop barrier
fuck you full of love. Sunrays (– 2) packed into
a glue-gun you fidget about with full of hate dive,
cascade, but not on

       your life or not.
       The effect
       is this.
Roger are you there. There is no-one touching my skin,
no-one touching my face. 98% of life there is
no-one I mean. The happy one submits that what we
need is the smirked exit from historical analysis
into a meaning caricature, bits of

       burlesqued metaphor and
       good turns

freed between the lines. E.g., Dribbling trotters
             on the treadmill like a tick say *polemic* –
night of my life, fell Ixodidae scream
             up it
is not passing but mainly ylinks&p=% faded yet
             alive and kicked –
funny enough you know, as you hang out the washing
             to 18.18, manual/ap
that this is the earth and heaven is on it
             (CABINET) –
even though it is only the morning at the moment.
                         You could be significantly
                         less expensive.
The hot news spread, out like a fire. Everyone which
I knew could see in down the passage stolpern and me
however, to I didn't Obacht during one. Two
horses three cops and the towering black with the
two-speed elbow all vanish. Alum, Borax, aller
frantic to know who and where I am and also what I am
eating you for Sergio. What product the news
will be is what you will ask, and asking for it
must die, with your frostbitten anus round the ceramic Lassie.
It will be more customized and higher quality.

Trust no-one suspect everyone let's get up on with life.
Antimildew additives as fuck. So even to
be happy that means not by 500 affiliates but by slitting
up the mirror is a lazy trick, bones fuss about in your hand
like spandex in a donut. TDI. Working this closely

with a premiere national news provider for the
majority of our news/talk stations makes you get
in the picture. Remember Adorno on *Oberflächenbedürfnisse?*
Remember life on acid? John Hogan a dispensing head for the
polymer crisps peanuts hats and whatever chardonnay,
                         did I ever say
how much I love you for. The sense put in
it is overwhelming. You can take that squirrel ornament
out now Albert but only if you want. The foam bun
life the invariable core tune, cantabile and you
be less whack – unequivocally to rise up as you hot up,
for the production of a part-rigid insulation music thing.
It all started to the meringue.
                              But fuck all that,
            why run
            up your debts and down your hole
            – *sit*
snug in the envy slit and a think. Near to the end
of the night with the litter everywhere and empty tin
sounds and smoke wallowing in the bubble bath
it was only cathected negation and me left.
What the fuck could we do next except learn from it.
Then, the helical slash screwed-down mint at
the base of the sick bag shimmers like adrenaline, and I know
                         all my
life is possession, and possession I know is a lie,
                     the wind
then feeds into the incredible flirting exhaust pipe,
                         i-amb
DIY dark blue vault redecorated a kind of mauve by
                     0.1

percent rise in the celestial dough called News Corp.

                        stick it to

me you

                        savvy begrimed porno caudipteryx,
so much I bleed, in a sense transcending even 39.74 in
a sense. He is the human appurtenance of the Neocon revolution
and all the appurtenances are available for data organization
choking out useable error margins in the freedom reading
by any means optional in the revisionist stock uprising.
Clean me. Teeth / nails add cop Exchange%2 equals obedience it
are you going to get out of your sleeping bag and
look left and right at the anti-mirror with your
hand containing a toffee hammer or not. It is
Christmas. And in any case you should get out more.

TORTURE LITE

Candied *faits divers* in frosted crackling, hurl myself
myself-mud immaterially scoffing up my fig
leaf face in a panto breakfast of hallucinations,
eating e.g. the "organ failure" niceties, August 1st
2002 *ex libris* U.S. Dept. of Justice, beneath it
all desire of oblivion runs out and is indifferently replenished,
or runs up another fine mess of print called nothing
worse than *a bill* or a reminder notice, iambic,
– then,

smear that mud in an Oscars of libido-backed rash
tutting also to be eaten, or eaten for,
farcical parataxis on heat and / or low heat, taking care
suck off my hands, grace to get it under the
dumb eyelids and *commedia non scritta* in the stretching
cheek torn up about all this crying

> please no wait
> Il Dottore I: The Sex Mishap
> pillar of the human

arrangement II:

> pleased
> no / wait /

you that security is an indispensable pillar of
salt-lick you can make anyone say anything
the Blunkett-Clarke horse, a balaklava in your Yakult
spine cooler, *listen to this chatter* –

- that men do not forfeit
- who claim that we hate
- if so,

the limit of honor in order to protect the freedom
Välkommen till Svensk Energi! *den is a country of*
endless possibilities. The classic defence is
the ticking bomb scenario: the ticking box scenario
comes *before* and *after*. Who do not sleep
under your oppression and diol. The squirrel ornament
is replaced: you remembered. And the helical
duck lays back and thinks open its polyurethane fundament
that makes foam guts spill on it and scratching a
noise but why, but fuck, all that. Pressing the gas with
her foot vanishes. They wrapped him in the flag
of Israel

                         Spavento, Meo Squasquara
                         XI: The Sex Is Right
        an arrangement
                  we can come
       to sure,
                  with strobe lights on
       for him MC:
                  out his hair / or not
sing Albert for all your life sing the dolphins fairly
mutter in their tank. Not without practising
I don't. And if Sergio were Michael Levin? But
he isn't in a bad state of permanent emergency.
You know when you were a kid you would smack
any person who pissed you off but you are now better off
and it is that special time of year. In the ear
soup some unthinking *fonctionnaire maudit* tips a shit
load of L'Oréal, the foreign insurgent snorts up
the shit-like incense of his own fanatical skin cooking,
Larkin in the air, the net curtains nailed down.

What did the plates and screws say to the counterculture?
Long sufferance is your Strepsil and your Flaubert.
In orgasm is your issue hexylresorcinol E131 and ham?
Long suffering babies chuck AIDS at the corporate pram lounge.
Lining up like inflatable beads the sectarian sky parts
                    its face to do a swallowing noise
                    at the Luke lightning, which
                    in turn scorns to answer flies
                    away and we the
                    bite down hard: Filing for a gracious
recount to ten or
                    a hundred then shout coming ready
or not. Includes 4 each ¼" and 20 × 1-⅞" pancake head
carriage nuts impersonated by the duck at the end
of the night grimacing as his privates disperse for 4.99.
Bitter experience but not sour, if you taste what I mean.
On the grate of a network of brass, made hollow with
boards to tread with care there must combust and fume
a wind-up dithyramb. And let go. The recipe is
amazing it can eat itself and chew your ear off,
                    the sound made
                    by this drowns
out the sound you hear it as, in the must-own life over
which the bisque vault and its asbestos clash, and in
which the indexed flavours of your eyes do
                    wasted in a saccharine
recount make the pluckiest outburst – . All life too
short to ride wait here. But there is plenty to do,
                    Fight or flight or
                    both way
                    better than either

one is alone. In the alcove there was a small semicircular
counter where one could buy franks or milk. To put
you simply know who you are dealing with it. Milk only
for the ancient baby thrown into Aristotle and Socrates,
scraping its honeycomb gums over their retired jumpsuits.
Bang goes my Friday night. To get down Sergio
would rise to avoid having to be hypnotised by the tray
of lobsters he alleges eats him. You can almost hear
that in the background. And under that brush
there there lies a filth of recrimination not slid through
lather on the salted red Calippo how does he
deal with or without it, your choice. Personally I slide
everywhere for my spine is tantamount to a flaming
toboggan loaded with the special contraband
of the negative, and Sergio you are beautiful is what I think.
You know what I mean by the negative on credit.
The duck section comes later. We were poor
but radical and made more radical by being poor
than you were. And silence is more silent than your
voice is but both in wet biro dry swiftly, taking your hair out
for a good time with friends round the block,
                    coming home to roost. Then 4.99
                          it is. I touch
                          another drop. Sign
                  my balls up for the blood diffusion
                          (not a *forte*, remember)
                  pet cause abdominal
                              cramp pet white
light out,
                  turmeric white su salud y
made for retina Tippex screams into adverse vinyl
chloride all way to bank. Helmet S.

Germinal: congratulation from AOL leach to ground
water optimum not first volatilised Brasso set on
your marks rubbed out. That is the revolving
door that is the way we get through it, lighting on the word
our to say *our* tanks perambulate through
                                    Westwood again from
                                    the east *i.e.*
Texas. Blue tongues on buzzers. You count and
recount the disrupted sporophyte of cabbage you are,
I am ours. Bite down soft. Over breakfast a Frida
Kahlo or Käthe Kollwitz print may as well dangle drilled into the
                  wall too
                        deep with its rivets not revealed
                        but you know they will be.
And Androcles slapped shut the mouths of mere lions,
and two peoples will be divided up from your body,
minuscule dextrin and carnauba wax rissole, plus gum arabic,
you don't live with a freedom deficit you die for it.
And the net tax loss in Fallujah, for what
it's worth in cremated sparklers is an immolation,
baptism of candida by yoghurt in the Hecuba
mpeg not for rewinding. With the toffee hammer
in your hand nail up the congratulation from AOL leach to
und water optimum not first volatilised Brasso set on
your marks rubbed out. Spavento screams that the critical twist
will this time blaze in a mark to market horizon, secreted
in an exploding foam bun hidden beneath the
skin of the day but always on a bad skin day
and strapped to the waist of a splitting duck
whose lids bat atavistically, whose dream work here is done.

*   *   *

21:53:40, and a letter from Banque Commerciale du Burkina
I discovered unclaim sum actimel rotted in
the bleached sun brightly as the stray police skipped by,
how we go strange and die, and stranger yet,
intimate with them all ghosts and dog fossils and all.
But can you despite that later go at strange eating
by Virgilian numbers the apples, chestnuts, pressed cheese roll and call
waiting out across the vast, flip that shit aisle in
between cress and rocket over. Sit there, play
without your food. Shed light cackling away this ethic.
And Dr. Akin Salif is back and talking about the Burkinabe treasury a lot
and Sergio is watching the chopsticks' striptease
pale in its abstract comparison and all the wankers choke,
buy into the night screaming 60% remittance.
Respectable terror matches an atrocious terrorising
quiet word for loud the immediate transfer according
to you agreed percent. And faithfully Mrs. Agatha DeBoer
                          cuts the waves –
                          pricks up a dogear –
Hydrolyzing Margaret Thatcher. After the war
baby actimel desists jittering in its gold
syringe like a sky angled to deep Maine ideally.
Hungry as my vein gets I can neglect it,
                          I am over love and over
eating out the window
                          burnt up and washed
away then home. Irving next up for "the metal hot from"
                          boiling Sprite up
next down in
                          the full mouth says
S. Germi how to complete level 4 tip sso se 6%

look a zero missing. How mimetic of you, – . Just going on
                    their nerve endangered
bees stoop past the emetic already recalled anyhow!
                    No respect, for life.
Now, the duck section in the epode (which was given first) is a bit
obscure but does unwind into a meaning you
can own: *splitting* is a pun on *sitting,* and
the duck is splitting because he has a bomb strapped to his waist.
The bomb is symbolised by the *foam bun,* which is
a kind of packaging equipment sold by Foam
For Comfort Ltd and Craft And Hobby Foam (CAHF).
But why a duck.
What the fuck do you think you are.

FOR CATEGORY \"A"\ WINN
                    It may not help
but just might if I tell you that the section about the net tax
loss in Fallujah is a joke about sacrifice.
Do you get it. Because if you throw everyone out
of a city you can't collect tax from them any more
can you and that is the joke. It would be a weird sacrifice offered by
                    the Iraqi treasury
wouldn't it. The imagery matches up with that theme:
sacrifice has often involved burning things, as in
the Bible on a brass grille or network of the kind I mentioned
back at the beginning. Hence the *sparklers;* but you might
say that sparklers aren't much of a sacrifice
                    to burn since, after all,
they're *meant* to be burned – but that's the crux of the metaphor,

just as well played backward as forward, just
as well stood back from as stood for, its switch is red hot
at the ON end like a titillated coolant and red hot
at the OFF end like a convention on rights. Combatant
humans standing for Darth Vader standing for
the zips of Qiaotou standing for Chihuahua diarrhoea
standing for a Wall's Mini Milk: open your heart.
You can get them from Kaboom and US Fireworks and
Wedding Things and HFM Pyrotechnics online.

Item No	Item Title	Case	Item
* sp10	#10 Gold Sparklers	44.00	5.63
sp14a	#14 Gold Sparklers	35.00	2.25
sp20	#20 Gold Sparklers	48.00	3.00
sp36n	#36 Gold Sparklers	69.00	4.50
sp08	#8 Gold Sparklers	35.00	4.50
us1003	Crackling Sparklers	56.00	14.25 *
ssp0981	Morning Glory 36"	132.00	2.25
us1005	No 10 Uncle Sam Gold	56.00	14.25 *
us1006	No 10 Uncle Sam Multi-Colored	56.00	14.25 *
us1007	No 8 Diamond Gold Sparklers	56.00	14.25 *
us1008	No 8 Uncle Sam Gold Sparklers	56.00	14.25 *
us1009	No 8 Whistling Sparklers	56.00	14.25 *
y28-003a	No. 36 Century Gold Sparklers	64.00	4.50 *

Mayhem: your beret. The small rain split up on a grid of thumbtacks.
And Rex Dickson is back and is Otutunzu Aguleri.
Then shift down into the ethic fallacy, racing
the shore off to the red ribbon, on stuff your face strike.
Pape zero aleppe: none of this is always what
you eat to survive, surviving to sing
a new tune all about having none of it: something
understood not fit to be wasted on understanding,
not brittle in the crammed mouth sick of air
but instead flatly indisintegrable, banished by love
and its sweetest decree to the fringes of red anti-gut,
where love alone shines in beauty, and the liver
waits agape on brass for its flame, and is licked
forever by that flame like a mirror by your eyelids.

HOT WHITE ANDY
2007

For Us

"*Que l'on soit difficile et que l'on choisisse au sein de l'abondance …* nothing could be simpler."

de Sade

Love deepely grounded, hardly is dissembled.

Marlowe

• A

Lavrov and the Stock Wizard levitate over to
the blackened dogmatic catwalk and you eat them. Now swap
buy for *eat*, then *fuck* for *buy*, then *ruminate* for *fuck*,
phlegmophrenic, want to go to the windfarm,
Your   • kids menu lips swinging in the Cathex-Wizz monoplex;
Your   • face lifting triple its age in Wuhan die-cut peel lids;
ng pick *Your* out the reregulated loner PAT to to screw white
chocolate to the bone. The tension in an unsprung
r trap co
          →   The tension in an unsprung trap.
                ck QUANT unpruned wing: sdeigne of JOCK
                of how I together grateful anyway I was
                Its sacked glass, *Punto*
                              →   What is
be done on the sly is manic gargling, *to*
to blacken the air in hot manic recitative from a storm throat,
WLa-15 types *to* Tungsten electrodes Aaron Zhong,
feazing that throat into fire / under its
hot life the rope light thrashes in its suds, [is] *Your* chichi news noose
/ Dr. Unicef Cheng budget slasher movie hype on *Late Review*
I keep dreaming about you every single night last
night I you making love Stan, I didn't know him then
it hurts, and *I* disappear but the nights stick.
Abner Jon Louima Burge Cheng.
          →   Ab … *etc.*
I am adaptable for Binzel and Lincoln and Panasonic
my swan neck my shielded arc, my gap of hot fire
Lavrov sidesteps in the long arabesque of equivalence. What is

being this lids clampdown, being this cheek slant
onto something, being this duck breast implant
but what is there
                  to eat in a specific fang,
                  defecation being otherwise a welding helmet,
                  being a gas lens,
                  being this hot skit spilt on glass
eat all of me like a dispassionately incinerated fish cheek,
I want being phonic into your intestine, to cry
into my own blistered eyes on the inside of your stomach,
not dead as the sea but cracking; disjunctive part
lives will then cancel the asymmetry of self-inclusion,
each of them will have the whole of love in it.
You witness protection flourish as autonomy, CPA Order
Number 22, Camp Bermel, hot white Vietnamization et. al.
Things change. Outside, people are different.
Lavrov becomes fraudulent. He and Johnson
Lee no fuck you. Then everyone necks the gouache to
dream her own acid scavengers, dream his own blood
        geyser knotted to cream tied out
        horizontally as a tripwire between foot-spas.
        WANT HOT ANDY CHENG?
        Want the enormous tragedy of the dream?
                Last night I
                        of you very hard and
                real I have put my fingers
                      on you and your fa
            ce if you were
                    here Russ Cheng
I mocking the crap Peisistratidai at reflector Ningbo,
into dead right crunch up your debit *virtù* Baode,
we present a fist with the power of law. Poetic sound

bites down hard into the fire blanket.
The enormous blackened air strives on toward production
of the zirconiated stable arc, the price war in the mouth
of:

- a stupid inflatable thing "like to a bear."
  (*pw* symbolised by 3 gummy ribs: check http://lion.chadwyck.com/)

- Andrew Cheng
  (*pw* is the passion of the non-identical in metre)

Do not leave me for Stan whom you make love with.
Each time they manage to levitate back what happens is you
lose a life Hyundai and make the art screen go black.
Beyond all this the city glows in natural repose,
listening to *Winds of Change* or *Kindertotenlieder*.

           In an empty window love dead
    to the frame recapitulates its stare, you push
           it wrong flat lips to the dewy
    basin of tin and hang there, come wrong.

           You soften inside when
    it is all ok, mimicry of the subaltern
           love droid voice initiates
    longing beyond its own fallacy this time.

           The forward ruse, the bright
    air reflected in water, the calling
           features all defy lazy
    song in astriction and flick away the cumulus.

Hallucinate the glass to
push your best face through, making up
with anything
basin of tin and hang there, not gone.

You harden inside as
really virtuosic as wrong, avenging it
the small hurts
like cutting water, like blind eye curfews.

The tack hammer is infinitely merciful. Spread out in the
carpark on the seabed your part lives throw frisbees
about and unblock their genital oblativity; but
the repulsed foetus still in character fastidiously vomits.

• B

At the committee meeting I spotted a woman in light,
she drifted past the monitor, I remember that
they were showing *Bleaching Lenny*.[1] The snow was
even and undisturbed outside as we fingered
the tungsten evaporation boats and screamed shit.
Square snow blackened by manic recitative.
We turned to see The Enterprises Center relatively
waft up in the imperial Wuhan sky like fish smoke,
blinking, glittering in our eyes,
and he turned to me, Akinsola Akinfemiwa, and said
the woman you see in light is light itself—
the light of the world, its copula and armrest,
she is the fulguration, the axis about whom endless
birth of heart revolves in magic fire and in fury
you must make her love you. She is Andrew Cheng,
imperator of the sled, backstreet *lumen naturalis*,
acting CEO for the true-way arc of priapic boredom,
you must be the voice she falls in love to categorically.
But Akinfemiwa is a fucking idiot.
We outsourced the snow to the most important hill
flung it on the dogmatic helipad, we watched
in livid concentration as the sky, in pursuit
of the protocols for our overdue Borland Delphi haiku split in
two like a smitten Ramadi heart, tediously equivocal—

---

1   British reality TV show. Famous comedian Lenny Henry is caught on camera
    inadvertently bleaching himself, one body-part per week. In the final episode
    (8) of the series we are given to contemplate a morose Henry, by this point
    a ghastly supernatural alabaster from head to foot except for his (since episode
    7) quasi-autonomous scrotum, engaged in teabagging an unnamed but
    invidiously Chinese companion of unfathomable gender. Henry fails to detect,
    through the dark suck-hole in her latex Marsilio Ficino mask, the tiny hidden
    natatorium of *bleach* fashioned ingeniously out of an aluminium peel-lid from a
    peach yoghurt pot Henry dared to lick out in the first episode (2).

but was I perhaps wrong to be maddened by Akinfemiwa?
And how would I know? From the dream?
The shit we screamed drowned out the next show entirely,
Blacking Up Lavrov, the episode where Johnson
Lee and the Russians rub hands at the stupidity
of the gouache drinkers, gnashing on their intestines and fire,
listening to *Winds of Change* or *Mozart*.

                    But this is enough to
          be real with, have the basin tilt fat one
                         thing less to worry
          shove out of my mind that mimicry.

                    You soften inside when
          it is working sex to be canny and elegiacal
                         fridge stains across
          the linoleum do not stop to wrong you.

                    Longer than the contact of
          thought with loss the need for either
                         you not to fade or
          never forget but then the chalk you eat.

                    Stick glass in it,
          to insist that the trespass is real too and
                         that you can break
          shove out of my mind banning that.

You harden inside as
if there is nothing in it, all to be endured less
thinly at work on this
in nonchalant, feverish cooperation.

Love realistically abandoned by Andrew is not shit,
thin rain drifts like torn roofing across the palace
dancefloor and your ravenous white lips snap after it,
ravenous for white blood, queuing for the other face
amputation shut in in the flaming Nestlé beach hut.

• A: *Turbo*

The Zhejiang Hengsen rope light to the tortoise hash—
hot white passion to the chastushka in livid grout,
but not just *in* the grout, *really blocked* in it—
amity to the pyrite on the ironing board, what is
it for this rapture of transitivity, this equivalence hypodermic,
the infinity of desire? What do I spread for?
Long wind straightens unfinishable and equated sea.
Cracked shut. Disorder is the enemy of progress.
All distant objects are veiled in a species of bright obscurity:
omnidirectional scanning allows any Article
orientation provided the Article jargon faces the scanner.
As you know, this holds for Article 2 up.

     fig. (a)
           Article 2
           Article 3
           Article 4
           etc.

Retrogression beyond this is just dada to a brick wall,
heartsquirt and neoplatonic drivel about the origin.
Cheng necks: 1. your *Sex on the Bleach*. 2. your *Colostrum Slammer*.
But the rapture, what is its *negatum*?
                      It is whispers
Cheng the *Fetischcharakter*, not of commodities but of dialectic
itself see through the Moscow limo windscreen pyromantic
oxygen stew transmute watch it slavered by the Beijing
kosmos onto new eyes superstitious to their frotted core,
whoring the shut lids they claim merely to underwrite!
The Zhejiang Hengsen rope light to the tortoise hash.
You soften inside the *to*, harden in the craniofrontonasal Berkshire disco.

Disappointed AmEx to the phlogiston, or make up your own (using "to").
Each is delivered and to each,
transverse adamantine.
Unnecessary examples followed, gunned out from
the heterodyne *r* trap transhumanced into OTC peroxide argument,
cf. want to go to the windfarm.
Photoreceptors Against Cruelty to Landmines!
The Made-Whole Johnson Lee to easySaltMeInFire!
Rapture of Transitivity to Hot-White
Cheng swarms off demosthenizing on the double in double χαρα.
He always does this. You get used to it. It is
what brains means. You know, *brains*:
UNHCR Damascus budget slash, something must be
done, for starters say no to outrages upon personal dignity,
dispassionate Postpasséist antipasti. Abner Jon
Rib Bag UHT Honest Doubt Bungalows Cheng Jr.— pizza?
In the dream is it really obscure, that slide-rule inner
in slide-shadow fat cut a rect | iccant from fingers
exit round the car. Show me. Angular Des, you wish you had come
up with something cutting to say back to Cheng
at the time, like fuck you and your idiotic χαρα Cheng.
The car leaves. Coke into my ass through a funnel.
But I love you despite the boring terrorism
of particularity,
fading like parity,
ground spilled into water
cuff slung hot across the abraded
jar shows particul | me screams
me despite
me I love you, rope l
You are so running out of time. Run impressed rope / trap out of it.
Run.

Everywhere to run to, everywhere to hide
the salami (*soppressata*) of the body apolitic,
                    the ad in grout
                    says let me out
                    so do
                    now do it again
                    do it
Rojar shows up.

                    Let it all out.
                    Rojar.
                    You want to fuck (*buy, eat* etc.) him
                    so to begin
                    détourn some Lenin.
ONE STEP FORWARD TWO LIMOS BACK.
Rojar shows up.
"A patriot is not a missile." *Nihil Obstretrics Inc.*
ACA NEWS: POMO DEBT FLOOR RISK (TW).

Rojarus.

Rojario climbs to his knees,
divine afflatus of EN 1783,
inwardly he kens himself the deputy April soot shower.

ROJAR: A quiescence so fucking dead
             catchy the sky cracks up its earplugs.

VYSHINSKY: In the past I never locked any of my doors. In fact, I never had
             a key to my home. In fact, I never had a home. I was never able
             to have a home, nor a door. Homes, moreover, were in fact not
             capable of being had, by me or by anyone who was not me. And
             what was true for homes was doubly true for doors. There were
             no homes to be had and there were no doors, nor was there any

mechanism for locking. In fact, locking was an absurdity. And if locking was an absurdity, locks were twice the absurdity that locking was. Homes then not being capable of being had were if anything still less capable of being locked, which in any case was an absurdity which was in no case so gross an absurdity as in the case of homes. Keys were shit. Now I understand I live in a very secure area, but ever since the attack I find myself making sure all the doors of my house are locked before I go to bed. Or even after I go to bed, when I am most asleep. Every time I do this I wonder, What is it I am afraid of? And sometimes, Am I afraid? I wonder what I am afraid of and I wonder if I am afraid. I am afraid of sticky damage and of invasion. But am I afraid of them? I mean, is it I who am afraid? Could it not be just a part of me? And am I afraid? I am afraid of the Cheng bubble, of Cheng futures, Cheng chic, offshore Chengs, of Cheng penetration, Cheng derivatives, of being wrongly Chenged, of war between the affluence nerds and the bliss nerds, of Cheng laundering, of One Night Chengs, of a chalk Bo Derek, of 7-11, of a miniscule 7-11 concealed in a special Yngwie Malmstein Signature version of Duchamp's *Hidden Noise*, I am afraid of Chinese whispering and orientation talk in the evacuated Houston Death Star, of the rogue Cheng, of laying waste my powers, of shattered glass on kidney, of being bent over, of Cheng's skirt length theory, of parallel Chengs, of the emerging Cheng with an impossible lock in his stomach which my hand reaches for despite me clutching a key made of terrifying crimson shit which erupts in flame and burns my fingers away to freezing yellow ash, I am afraid of the seven figure Cheng in one state of mind. But is it my life, and is it a homage to bathos? This is the first year I have been asked to wear a name tag at school. Anyone visiting the school has to be temporary in order to enter. Both Tommy and Benjy Cheng warned us when our nation was brand new. They taught us not to let fear change what we could never better believe in.

CHENG: I melt the glass with my forehead.

STAN: Who is this prick holding up the placard for Stan.
Stupidity is the glass ceiling of decathexis.
Which is frosted in Stan at the personnel door.

Philosophy is what makes you feel
whatever you feel truth is.

AKINF.: 'Widerspruch Sprach Frei: The Oedipol Duplex With One Back.'
(draft version)

Who cares if the President is blown by his intern,
so long as he doesn't macerate the innocents.
Or vice-versa.

CHENG: l'objectivation infidèle des producteurs…
la survie augmentant selon ses propres lois…

STAN: Who is this.

Frost.
CHENG: In fire and vinegar swings the total beige,
thinking in a roundabout manner and by means of bricolage.

CHENG: We can only try to love ourselves as wholly as possible,
to love ourselves unconditionally, in bed and in debt,
forsaking all others.

You know, thinking: Unangemessenheit, erection blues.
So Cheng shows up at the poetry reading,
looking ridiculous like some bleachaholic Ethiopian queen
on a crap metabathos trip, scorched scraps of tightrope for sandals,
you wouldn't fucking believe it, I mean
what kind of ontological AC-DC thinks he has to wear black
lipstick to hear Joan Retallack? And who cares?
There were hot milk flecks on his bougie mouth anyhow,

Afghan diamonds in the rapture of the strobes.
So anyway we listened to *The Reinvention of Truth*.
It was some brilliant adumbration, Romantic propositivism
left in the wing for dust, live and postresistible,
quiescence a Cage could at best have dreamt of.
In fire and vinegar swings the total beige.
But Cheng totally ruined it. After necking his Diet
Styx and smacking his aflame lips he staggers
up and grabs the mike, condemns the whole
phalanstery to his performance poetry, some kitsch Ovidian thing
Raytheon and Erinys, bathotelescopic beyond belief,
literally, then some thinky retro poetical work in progress
full of *you soften* and *you harden*, all that fashionable
legless jackbooting of the abstract second person, inevitable
prosodic botox as *points de capiton*,

- inevitable hackneyed sex negativity
- inevitable recusant lyrical I
-   "   " muzakological *Coucher du Roy* klaxon solo
-   "   " UNHCR Damascus budget s

etc, until finally this hot white Cheng-scenester
But I live in imperative sympathy with you. Put down her
drink and ran •
to the front. Ran up to Cheng. Y
You in a red dress in my dream, being the entirely beautiful.
The tension in an unsprung trap. I am grateful
I am grateful You stay.
Russ ran to Cheng, thinking
you know she She is for my only life impossible
to pull out from
my heart, my fingers snap bleach snaps,
farce is the third term and is perjury incommensurable with sex.

You will not repeat this but will repeat not repeating it
my dream, yrrour of my mazed head,
The Zhejiang Hengsen. The workers for the Olympics
from Kent
• ht *eines* gilt dir, Fiasco Chong, Cyclone Shredder Chong
g Diamonds flaring glasse, | lost to Hebei
grateful any KENTSOFT / HEBEIHARD
to *Fin.* to him and said

My bed is that by the window.
I speak to my bed. Your sheets are alexithymic
throat fat that rocks flirt under,
I get to them risking the intensity out of my life.

I am into communicating this,
you are this right and dead in the ear
that there is a deeper peace crackling under,
and right in the head that spit love out.

My bed is that by the ceiling.
It circles it like you, a lunacy of dust
that squared with a mouth in total lust
you had better quickly scream about.

You soften inside when
eat the same restaurants and be together said Mr. Mustapha
You harden inside when
Brushroll___Agitator_Parts_565.html stop trying contact

I wait to communicate this.
Take my face to the window doing next what
now you do. I need
but will not have you, go instead crassly skeletal.

Again.

My bed is by the window.
I speak to you. You are impossible to forget,
the face ecstasy screams under,
lighting the world you damage and repossess.

I am communicating this.
You undiminishably are what I mean by all
love defiant under
the shadow of a dispassionate end in the right head.

I go on without you.
Impossibility mitigated by the comedic brake,
on loving to square that
mitigation with the future hermetic sex square.

You soften inside but can't,
submission is just the disquiescence of the ecstatic scream.
You harden inside but at
last can't, it is simply pointless to live without that light.

I wait to say this.
I now say it, without you to your face and without
knowing how stupid is
my desire for the next big thing: CHINA.

But simply pointless life in sum is the continuum like any other.
Lavrov and the Stock Wizard levitate. Flaring
glass will wipe your eyes, will learn you self to cherish,
in fact but you are rightly tender always. Really you
are whatever follows, whatever loss unspared. Pointed hints
of the Industrial Zone are collaged at risk of
your lips bricking hot wrong into the soda gap, livid white fire
pipes up about my teeth and guts and open door,
its hot shielded arc red with dilemma. Your tenses are
        the wanting of desire
        your tenses are the wanting of desire
        [later: the *wanton*, then *won ton* of desire]
dysphagic rollmop Kebton Akinfemiwa fuck at last can't their
violent snow

                dying to turn yellow
                in warm light / next wave of A&E closures
                living to turn blue
                in the hot white blur of living screwed to
                fat throat recto
                an army without culture is a fucking dull-witted army
                correction
                an army without culture is fucking a dull-witted army
                rose-tint auroral fistfuck
light points your face at the news. The flaring glass is visualised,
and at last the phantasmatic oesophagus is fed out through it: shatter
me shatter me screams the ski lift at

　　　　soap the equated sea dream up the scam
　　　　live up the dream
　　　　how like you
this finale to the whole Chang question the whole problematic
congelation of hot genitals wrapped in the *Houston Chronicle*
to crack its metaphysic ad banner. In white out
your tenses are the wanton of desire, gazing through the
Xi'an YMCA window at The imitation Gap lit up scampi-eyed
desire krush ex necromat it lives my own way,
soft hard soft hard soft, skewered by Metulla and Kfar Kila,
and other names besides, names to know and do.
I accumulate you: sky crated in Binzel and 'Change, crated in illumination,
I accumulate you: hot sky deserted by Abner and tax phosphor.
The superpower to come is love itself. Articles 2
up and the Antepasséist 0. But since this is my only life
I accumulate you Andrew Lumocolor, not fit for waiting
away uptight in fire shopped to spit, but a real man
accumulating men, desire and intensity until I die.

STRESS POSITION
2009

Stress Position I: The Question

"Obedience doth not well in parts"

For Deborah Katz

This is the honest account of the passion of Ali Whoever, read it
deep in the words, general Vampire, fashioning from this trance
    in mental colours an idiot life to blank, taking the time that
declines to rhyme in synchrony with yours, conscious forever
    of limits and where in the end they lie, general Jurisprudent,
the limits to meaning and power, and as innumerable stresses rise
    in a pyramid of lyric ash and flame, keep your eyes out.

•

This is the justification, inflexibly worded, of the screen test
of Lucas Manyane Fritzl, leaping on strings up the escalator
    but going backwards, his crutches in knots, grace of hallucination,
Joey you say jump or better scream it but a swivel is all
    he makes toward reality, your place, general Echo
Gas Hedge Trimmer, to softly retort, his lips dripping in floating
    rate notes and perpetuities, *The void is grounded in the free.*

•

Forgetting whatever he means, stroking the cartilage of general
Ice-Belt who elopes with gravity, flush to the infinite
    turnstile filling in for the otherwise vacuous mouth of the prompter,
where the decisions are made, sounds like questions: if the so-called
    void is grounded as Ali let slip in the free, who owns the grinder,
and who are the traders who ration its daily grind, if not me?
    Sunlight on the stair points out the T-wall, drowned in life.

•

This is the movable end of the poem. What it allows you to do
is stop right now, whenever you've had enough, you just return to this
    stanza and hit *think this*, an art-fix panic button,
and the outlying mental travail will expire and lift, the cryptic plot against
    the earlobe become blatant, frigid ordnance recant in the sky
in general and NAME 8 split up retool CIPHER 3 just fuck and
    run *what* BOX-SPRING 5 *t* get out BLANK 1 this is the game on

•

Right of the stem, honed to unclassified backfill, scantily held
in tight by later eliminated fingers, GUTS 6 static
    not slopping out on the new mosaic, shines in the mind and heart
of the open Al-Rashid, you will pay? And fill the waters
    that slick the eponychium with futures and remains,
parting their leg? Right of the T-Wall fondling its squandered animal
    peristyle, will FRONT 8 get that feeling-chewy feeling?

                                    •

Our allegory beds in where political will undeletes its remainder
who think outside the border, votes with its feet to recycle the emerald
    pedalo slang, surrogate socialized medicine, atomic dyspraxia
down the laddered words scratched in lost ash there slides a rumour,
    cashed out to a mirror, over the river relieved by eyes
by forgeries of SEX 6 rise up bloated in bathypelagic
    Sorb-it CONE-FACE 4 or its stunted double to crack on reflection.

                                    •

Shit for yourself. LEG 8 flung at the hadji depressor alleges
beams rip the superior oblique, pointed in by the domestic
    help who connive to blind FRONT 1. The apocryphal teeth for TEETH
3 fitment salvage by moral dicot the icy *yes* or yes to
    10 is how far, and what in the end is acceptable unto Taha
Bidaywi Hamed as a biometric ID pun? For redistributing
    the skin of a vaguer animal to dye its underside disgust black?

                                    •

Whatever you say. What will the lung at LUNG 6 flatten into
incendiary dust and cloud if by the sympathomimetic adverb
    ok LUNG 4 is upgraded to a trip hammer? And if at the corner
whose could it is what if the platoon has cancer? Deeper tissues,
    stickproof and subterogenic, scrub up void. To extract like a cheek
of a balloon dog that, if you rub it on wool, you can cuff to the radiator
    colloid? Up in the air the statelier animal rights in colour

                                    •

Detonate into the galaxy wastefully riveted over the payload
in love with its predestination, trailing its nimbus of backfiring gore,
   umflattert sie tausendmal, careering to posthumous outer space,
stuffed with intelligence, archly declining to parody turning back
   the spit whose uncookable data redacts itself to the perfect lack:
Why I Left CONE 7 Alone in Custody of the Circular
   Saw with Nothing but Undefrosted Arteries for Alimony

                                    •

   For Idiots, or *How to Get Expat Cimmerian Swingers to Fling*
Caution to the Desk Fan and Sing the Instructions to Pat its Plug In, or
   Time on the One Hand, Blood on the Other: Backrubs for Ventriloquists
with Pretensions to Preternatural Thromboembolism. Wherever I go
   whistling after you, swinging the collar, GUTS 2 interfused
with counterfeit CONE LUNG 8, must it be always because the way
   back in from SEX 2 fucked dead is an impossible uphill slog?

                                    •

   The edge of our middle distance adjusts to glimmer in ethanol,
I a conscientiously synthetic boutique koskin crop in PVC
   bath water, strip to my gated pelvis, scorning the rhyme for HEAD
2 I split HEAD 5 I what HEAD 8 I emptied of valuables
   bracket psychosis, egging reality on to abolish the start
salted in blatant desire, bound for its last incompressible shallows,
   where overflow is seepage *in flagrante*, back to you.

                                    •

   The pessimists do not know what to do. However the honest
reprise of a glottal catharsis dipped in ringtones and croton oil,
   Ali Whoever's total windpipe asset management wipeout.
Passion in draft, circles in profile, what they prepare you to do
   without is the shattering innards ratcheted up in incurable flame,
to get by instead on epigastric larceny, latterly coming in second
   waves for the sucked-up sky to crack, assimilate and fake.

                                    •

CONE FACE 5, square to the death. The Outback IED
birthday lock-in editor comes free with the supraorbital
    lyric lock-in editor, thundering words at the rivers of blood?
What if that candidate is wrongheaded? And if GUTS 4 prone
    on the mattress of balloon animals looks askance, expecting too much
downtime off the riveted back and sides? To know ourselves diseased
    is half our cure but less than half their least, worried phantom?

                                    •

    What's an arc in the spine? FRONT 8 shutdown, miracle liver
function normal, drink your teeth, on for the savage reliving
    as *at what* price, *what* fixing. On the meniscus of sweat
curved on LIPID 1 that bankrolls what, under the plating
    bath 4 into that? SEX 2 its thing? The precision No Vac blasts
the strangulated loophole out the wedding, playing possum
    with the baby placated in FACE 8, not with the vampire bats.

                                    •

    Right of the empty tree, burrowing into the screaming person
reconstructed out of boot polish and Actimel pots, fired at
    lipid LIPID 9 *what* variable stem length? Wet katyusha
dry up with the bloodshot steam, out for the hooded on switch
    in the whisper? Who will then divide the sky in two and run
down the batteries lodged in breaded soil, looking to try
    scraping by on saliva, accepting the crunch, renditioned awake?

                                    •

    The year sets in as the anime scions of Guru Ali Goraknath
flanked with Fijians fold into a Tetra Pak for bad acid liquidity,
    as, first lifting your eyes, you stomp the Pak flat, abruptly for
whose metaphor licks at the sole of LEG 6. Ash kissing delisted
    FACE 3 holographics shining, into the park where
the quiet animals are under the stairs, moving their secret lips
    in sync with the quiet screaming dots on the glass, where later

                                    •

They go frigid when you embed them. Lost beneath the shower
head of their flesh in the market dark, mockery *fort et dure*
    but TEETH 5 pats its forgeries ripped out the scar built in,
be careful not to use desire on this. Irrespective
    dusty teeth and washy tyres, hours, the hot specifics,
the hand over Paul. Redistributing the intelligence of the sky
    as you sing and of the winds as they interrogate the thinning

                                    •

Interrogated CONE LUNG 8 flattening yes in connoted
pyramidine who dances, under the ironic M2T training
    and what is accepting it for? In the bathypelagic food-grade
melody spun in the emerald sound is stripped, later erotic
    fly zone GUTS 3 stripped, meta-erotic in what you hear
stripped, flung at the levator, reversed in a panic of interest
    static to replace sound, which is too often lying and wrong?

                                    •

I walked inside that room and saw as the night shears forward
flung at my back I knew you sitting there the ground upon
    a base of shadow caught like tinder over watered people
grew into the flickering heel I threw around the sky
    whose music strained to a beautiful agony out of my ordinary
steps to be at your side who sitting there are as I never knew
    was you until your head turned and are you in breathless air.

                                    •

Symmetry in us sped then whose hologram at last lost out
to live at impossible cost the ceiling dropped in shreds of ice
    sieved through plywood live and bleed in only one distress
bound to one flesh your unspeakable loveliness that now the dry
    air floods over only to rise back up as into catastrophic
music nailed to never comes one echo of our solitary
    body in that room bare of the only world but you.

                                    •

Right of the crater's tip, scuffing its eyelids on that eyelid
of uranium warthog, Bremer on the make in made-up life,
    vomiting terrorist rib, hedged, ramming its arrogant calories
in dark walled in by GUT, who is this person making faces
    at the faces of Jeremy Greenstock really for? Up the creek
of Zimbabwean irrigation, peddling powdered milk to burn,
    whose stuck imagination importunes the striving star?

•

The miraculous bar sets in, miles away in the futurist trailer
whose polyester axle wilts like genitals in jail
    FRONT 6 anything that can be rationalised blur into the straw
this open? LIPID 9 inscribe an icon of defeat? In
    SEX 8 cracked at last in the rectangle mind screwed into the wall
courtesy of its regenerate mascot, landmines in its pee
    bespoke ejaculation, animals only, to massacre 3?

•

Wash your mouth, rustle of sweetened Diyala afflicted with affix
FACE 2, affix CONE GUTS 6, the life you rifle down
    battered in sparkling blood and procrustean sewage, hardly ever
actually free karaoke? The revolving door that leads into the emerald
    has seven doors and seven plates of glass, the enabler who pushes
it round, owning the push bars, pushing its meaning inward
    itself is the spice of diglyceride notably drilling thought for oil

•

Like as in a pit of down, a gap inside the market
stuffed with human paste, unregistered cries of unlistening bacon,
    subject to the legal repeat of 'Bat out of Hell' 1, 2 and 3?
CONE GUTS 6: 'Bat out of Hell' 1, vacation in origin;
    HEAD CONE 3: 'Bat out of Hell' 2, bilateral orca;
huffing on FRONT 4 to raise the pyramid of embers
    deluging Sorb-it, LIPID 8: 'Bat out of Hell' 3?

•

Vous craignez que je ne voie pas assez combien je suis
out of the frying pan, into the choir of meat, ground to air
    I came in to decapitate my back. The rented piranhas
six-deep in the basement of lactic acid last liberated
    at the second of judgment to stand for anything, to go soft in
the head they chew companionably switched at the order of play from RP
        helmet to PR beret, as the erotic rotisserie floods?

                                •

    We went to this McDonald's where the theme was dialectic,
food with no way to buy it, lines at counters with nothing to eat.
    Al-Mansur took us there, shading his fringe from the radiation
of profit alive in the eyes of Ali Whatever who served our mayo.
    The secret of dialectic, he said, is song, the whole rendition
of living voice, the infinite modulation of pulse, the swell
    of severed lungs restored in lust of joining the roundel.

                                •

    At that we detected the restaurant floor was spinning, and we who
come to tread its dust were spinning too, not in our minds
    or on our own commission, so that we seemed to be standing still
like jilted dates at the now open weekends Al-Rashid, scanning
    for love like Bradley Manning. Al-Mansur turned, clutched at
my wrist, fixing my eyes with his, incanting then what must
    have sounded like this counsel, since it is what I remember:

                                •

    To comprehend the movement of this place, its great leaps forward
at counters for nothing to eat, the unpayable ransom of the happy
    meal you scorn, the flutes of Mavala Stop, their res mancipi
porn foil, you must liberate the void scored in its blur,
    crusade into its hallows in asylum, to its shrine to what
the idiots who work here think is power, but what you and I
    know is not power but justice, now disappear and discover this place.

                                •

The coterie of comrades looked at me, dropping flirtatious
shadows on the spinning floor, circular edge to edge,
        under the emerald bust of Al-Mansur, the hadjiavatis
who went up in a tortured flash of smoke, blackout at twilight.
        A new sensation cosseted the air, half of burning
and half of letting motherfuckers burn, inspiring credit
        surplus to insanity in meat, through flaring nostrils

                            •

        You know what you have to do, said the comrade with lips, and I did,
but the leg on the left of my right leg revolted, my left leg elected to jump
        and tossed itself off of the hip, landing in ketchup and straws by the bathroom.
We accepted this was what the Hudson intern dismissed as not a sign,
        in gratitude attaching our feedbags and their receipts to her CV as trimmings.
Pulling myself together, apart from the leg, I cast a long, waking
        grimace at my companions, and hastened away on my hop to the shrine.

                            •

        Weeks passed, as the counter help and security stood gaping
with mouths shut tight, hoarding their precious saliva from alien looters,
        implicitly cheering in silence my progress over the fourth wall
now underfoot, powered to spin in urgent, slow cascades.
        At my back I heard my comrades plot to eat each other,
waiting to let the words go down, throwing up their hands.
        But on the straight and solitary path I went my way.

                            •

        Abducted at no checkpoint, never yet exhausted, blood
gushing from my cratered hip in cursive wet balloons
        on to the floor where a twist of gut just now regurgitated
by a patron properly evacuated does for a mattress, and at last
        I gained the terminus at which my leg, locked in a progress
predicted by Al-Mansur before he abdicated, born to come
        back to now, whose fingers suddenly spring from the rim of my arm

                            •

Toward the door, pointing and playing their idiot scales in the air,
whose leg this was that brought me to this question, standing forever
in wires of lightning, bracketed whole, not disputing the debt
to the one gone, disfavoured knee tossed in the carnage of straws?
Mine and therefore mine alone I said, not at that moment
contriving to be heard by the black staff, nor caring at last if I should.
The laughter died away, the room was dark, and I reached for the door.

·

A child inside that toilet, my mother outside, my sister
with her there, I gaped from my spasming face at the graffiti
penis surrounded with frantic, scrambled confession, of neurosis
or just desire, fantasies knifed in the door, for hire, misspelt
I knew even then, stories of virtual Ali the cubicle frescoist
when suddenly skinheads walk in and kick open the door, drag my hair out
make me shit my pants, systematically gang fuck me

·

With their cocks, one then another, tendering soft excuses over
my head about me, racked in their denim and boots, their sick white skin
solecistic in the summer urine and the white breast stretched
in a warm list over the T-wall, fold-up mad albino plait push
into me I love you fill my guts restore my flavour
and if I walk outside she will take me by the hand and we will continue
into the town centre shopping passionately erect and tiny

·

This toilet is a spinoff Argenteuil of the Tigris, thunders Louis
Leroy fuck this wallpaper get back to the hadjiavatis no but
they must finish me. Suddenly they walk in and kick on the door,
my hair rips out, there is the fucking, happening to me,
face FACE 3 my open back whose cock is invisible clings to
love them you finger the lock on the door and smile. I alone will
forever dream the loss of you, my analgesic fascists.

·

242

Your in any case indistinguishable faces now melt into one.
I am the tiniest one and I know who it is but I will not say.
　　Stare out the infantile not yet bloodshot eyes at the penis cut into
this side of the door to demand it erupt in intensity to live
　　forever with, to rip out my newborn hair, screamed to oblivion.
In truth not life this looking is slow and infinitely gentle,
　　or if finitely, all at once with nowhere else to go.

•

　　At risk of less than any human death. The comrade pretentiously
allergic to torture, scratching his nappy rash, kindly now will finish
　　the shouting match rigged up in ersatz noise in the earlier stanzas,
will condescend to rise up to the roll call, bidding salvation
　　resume as we wait for the amputee to dispense with the diligence
due to the stubborn impediments to his door. General vampires
　　on the make will make allowance for obscenity honestly meant.

•

　　Reconstruct them. Boxing and frolicking FRONT 2 chit in shreds
of eye duct shit LEG 8, shoving T-walls up the class cracks
　　of the Council of Union, tucking TEETH 6 into blankets of GUTS
6 for a paradigmatic match. Cream soaks in the fire door
　　hinged in dingiest 5, kicking silicon FACE 3 at it,
just punt it like a football, thinking of birth and ruined cocaine.
　　Pewter, like a boom mic garlanded with trophy ears.

•

　　Reconstruct yet more of this arcade. Illogically SEX 5
stabbed up CONE FACE 2 makes sanity crawl out the mongrel nozzle
　　of LIPID 3, spattering the faggot alsatian on LUNG 5,
grinding in the logo for TEETH 9 who will embezzle
　　painlessly the tedious gist strung up in GUTS and Co.,
then chuck it out. Boot fetishists tangle with Ali all over
　　the upside down debt ceiling, fluctuate like pinball.

•

And when the reconstruction wraps up, then what? Black comedy
channel hopped to blanched-out antiphon, the subject in spite
  of remedy lives to see its cone dysfunction rule the world
out of sight and hardly mind, paralytic spasms on a sunbed,
    stuck in phenomenology, rotating mincemeat for eye holes,
blinkers for bliss. Nothing but pork and grits, the Pakistani
    Halliburton hireling snaps at the third asking, sensing the eyes

•

Hog-tied neo-platonically in his Kuwaiti handler burn into
his back in a panegyric to the moral of contract. I put my hand
    out to touch the door, saying aloud, this is the way
meant by Al-Mansur, through this door is the permanent static
    tornado, sheer white sound to supersede the lying round
we continue to file for, spent like lice in the petty aeolic scream
    of a hair dryer vomiting leftover lava, never devouring love.

•

The door swung partly sideways. Nothing moved. Where my working
hand had been was now a slot of lip. The surfaces of
    this lip slid, greyed. I had a stomach pain, it was okay
smash the door open. What limb suddenly was it once that had
    abandoned me to thrash in plastic spoons, for whose smile
was it ripped in Ali Tumnus, as with a clatter as of
    oil deep-fried in water just added he whispered, as you think?

•

Right of the door you open like that, blu-tacked to the major
accounts desk screwed down in the restaurant canteen, hovering high
    above the atmospheric dry ice pumped from fiscal paradise,
I saw a tiny wardrobe. Making as though to peel open its door
    I extended the lip of my arm. Tinier beads of sweat and icing
drift from a dispenser on the wall into the basket
    combatant I came in to redefine you back, you will do

•

what in my touch, castrated star, buffering indigestion
with longing, stoned most nights either to add or subtract varnish
    dead accurate, half-curious child pulling its own legs off
and sailing them in sex and wine, sticking pins in a lung
    to make the scream blow out, playing records over records
with the cube root of tongue, lived to go, pumped up like a pedicured
    foot on the neck to nowhere, where death is gold leaping

                                •

    This end sets in, tallying up the registered shouted body parts,
the sections of narrative, logic aborted to fit with its fantasy trial
    run for a shaded career as an OHRA security detail,
the spinning floor, all the commentary on Meat Loaf, the love lyric,
    everything been and done and all too late to pull out now,
but there to live and deal with, finished in language unrelated
    to the speech of lining in the only throat still here, and how?

Stress Position II: The Workings

"Prodigious birth of love"

To the anagrammatic Diotima I am a bare intuition of Vietstock
so we split—on a skiv run down the Street like a milky gutter
    of burnt silk singing 8000 BAHT the girl with the waggly tail
my eyes too. A billion negligible eggs in a rectangle pruned
    to a triangle, pruned to a dot. Making the parts of a sky inside
you shift, think, you too, reliving Svay Pak. Across the road
    Tajik scag, *Satyr* alive on theft, metanarcissism.

•

Repress the bass note buried in this fabric, idiot echo,
the ring in my burning ears, iron hot. In all it blurs
    whatever is left into everything still to play for, listed under
its metonym to carve into the artery under the counter
    where in sparkling spastic dance desires pierce a hole
to tempt in wandering feet. I go inside and shut the door,
    unfold the hiding place, and, soft, begin to stare.

•

The aim is self-sacrifice. Now looking down into
a woman laid out on her back I directly look into a hole in her foot.
    The foot is raised in the air, primed for intensity, I can't
understand how beautiful it is, my thin heart thrashes at
    the limit it sets to flesh in stone now flooded by brilliancy
later unknown, this is the real dot I hear my missing voice
    repeat to the shrinking air collapsing spinning to the floor.

•

Now I want that to be repeated back to me in white noise
livid with static in grey on the black market, disoversaturated
    like truth faded into. I fashion the hole in the foot into
a man I will call Dot, not a person yet but a multiple
    in glaring silhouette of whom it thrills me most to eat
like a chthonic donut which, licked on the sugar, tells us the story
    of my dot, of Black Beauty, of the gastro yacht, of poetry.

    •2

The real dot. The pond on the floor, the pond in the shade of the trees,
the actual Acteon barging into the airing cupboard. Voided
    noise adrift resembles human lowing, under the stairs, in
the dream above the head, a briefing on lust for the living inviolate
    5 or something, brink of wherever the trawler and fatty artillery
go yellow in their inflexible burlesque of standard operating reflex,
    pinscreen Corbièricules *vs.* the penis of the of bulimic Pacman.

                      •

Lines from a poem repeated until they replace the thing you mean
and hear by singing them first to last forever as they end.
    The last speck of SucraSEED glints on the vinyl, cold as grit in ice,
you watch it spin into a frontal impact with the cutting stylus. Nightmares
    in expressionism, never inherent enough to their prehistory,
veer into alien backchat, Ali, easily too far gone
    to return from afar, the Chinese burn on lyric square one.

                      •

The pond of clear water, the shadow laid down by the trees, the rushes
and bright water-lilies in sprays by all the beginning and end. The gate
    at the side in the fence, the dog, the creosote, the rain-logged pornography
yet a real beginning, in fact you love the dog, and even trust in
    the skin in the destroyed pornography with an indecipherable microscopic
dot in it like a pin hole to flood up the intensity to make love panic.
    The skin of the foot is a factual object of beauty, feel your orgasm.

                      •

The skin is in a boot on what? In this story, in the Chicago
of Kogelo under Elysium, where only the rotary door is archaic
    in circles and routinely ergonomic. But is my hunger
real enough yet to transact away reality for a certainty,
    the certainty that whatever I suffer is mine or that whatever
can love me too is absolute and here, and if it is,
    Black Beauty, why do I care how else it isn't yet, or where?

                      •

Particularly when, she agreed, you can rip up the air, and pointed at it
and in a scurrilous flash turned into a heap of intestines, then tying
    up her hooves behind her croup, did it again, again the same
flash, same heap, value, see, she said, and now watch this,
    and this, and bound her legs into a safety knot, tightened it with
her teeth and again the identity flash and void, and the question is not
    what it means but what it takes for sanity to crack.

·

The real dot. Somebody stood on a nail or over the pillow
over the nail I lay my sleeping head, untraceably loved.
    For the hiss in the airlock is only the muzak stimulus to echo,
anyone can mistake amateurish screaming for amorous screening, jerk,
    but not I am watching this dot forever and how it turns me on
like growing new a tooth, you have to finish me. If you see
    it means the vapour clotted in eruption dissipates.

·3

The time you always stopped and never had. Forbearing to flinch,
plastic iris, used to look into it, spotting their jump cuts, alienation
    ellipsis instructively left gaping, midriff in the garbage
burger continuity editing, boot-scuffs scored in the undressed
    bodies banked on the floor upholding a platter of moaning faces
boringly anonymous and congenitally all iconic, laid on for
    the ravenous mind like a rat trap, amazed, props to the shutter action.

·

I don't want to hear it, the monster rock epithalamion *verité*
flambée drowning in blue cheese, it's cancelled. Because just eating
    the platter itself is enough to get the purée backflowing,
anything on top of that is a deductible tribute to puritan gluttony,
    so that the dots are joined up into a skeleton already,
a skeleton wanked in public, emptily coating its showy darkness
    which spits life back in dust, cut with ground-up mirrorball.

·

But *kein Glück ohne Fetischismus.* At the same time nothing
without the blur you sing, having to surrender nothing
    to do nothing but only to wait for it to disappear by itself.
Whoever knows that better than anyone who actually had to do it,
    immortalised in famous words: the hadjiavatis who stands
for sacrifice whether it eats or is famished, for need whatever need
    aborts into or when you disappear, for passion in everything

·

Where you disappear. Donut! love this man. He is not only
the real me that he means by that expression too, but socially
    climbs into one less thing to worry about: bogus ligament
tucked in the oven defrosted long ago, you just missed it.
    But fuck that joke, really? We percolate down to the sea
and run out in permanent patterns, distinct, even spared the press,
    the loss leader left on the stand for hours stacked in days.

·

Warm on the frozen earth beside her pressing up into the tilt
of sky covered in mud with her and my beloved fingers and
    my shoes on I rock hard surge in joy inside her so beautiful
croup now credibly stripped across the triangle of cloud
    invented for this love you find a place over the patio
beneath the window through which they sit still and will watch anything
    on that night I lived there was the flesh of static flood.

·

The real Dot, staked to the burning wall, the liquid towel-rack
coating the head, a fist on the liquid knee, the one now bending
    bath in silence the door definitively locked in with me
points up at the octopus screaming look at the face on that
    in time calmly laughing the air bulging like a lost hair in
the stomach I flatten at infinite light I flash to cross into at
    the foot of the stair where lost for its ecstasy I see Dot in.

·

Dot is a cliché, recherché porn, gut and bifocals, French, or he
is the octopus, cripple studs, other who swallows his longing and drinks the boot
     polish reheated with broken laser arms, snaps, and is tattooed
in the bath the foot pushes, remembering in time he is only liquid
     love and is not real, a uniform tango, fuck you, flat-pack
like Pac his hearts are branchial his throat ersatz who never did
     stay till the end or come back forever but just drops you.

                                   •

Hakagawa, his back broken in headspins under the Graners,
reared to the noise of smacking lips, the rustle of civilized voices,
     9000 BAHT no plosive real world/rear word implicate scars
welded compliant restructured, wielded according to any delusion
     tested on ice, ratcheted up to wring the cortex dry,
seduces prepaid Dot back to his yacht, the General Stroop,
     not taking yes for an answer, swelling the idiot scavenger hunt.

                                   •

We board and relax on the scatter of tackle: CCCC, N,
S, VVV, and like neophytes rapped on the nimbus we open
     our cook books, which fall open at the first *données saignantes*,
raw data in English, nod, let's fucking eat. When it is safe
     to already know despite life what my answer will be, VC . . .
so that the risk, l'aléa, the uncertainty, the unstable
     compound knot in the tag on the sandy trigger finger snaps.

                                   •

     Ph. A little meat best fits a little bellie. *Ch.* Lebendige machen
alle den Fehler. *Ph.* Life is a symptom of arctic seafloor drift,
     sciatica butting in on the orgying supertweeters. *Ch.* L'éveil
blanc des phosphores chanteurs. *Ph.* Cashmere eyelids, heed the white
     beauty singing what. *Ch.* Tôi làm con búp-bê nh_y/hàt
Ph. drift, Narodnost barging *Ch.* arrested wheel, fly the yacht
     Ph. spilt, guttering to light *Ch.* make up the difference *Ph.* The deck

                                   •

Jerked, jumped by the currents, and was swept forward, tossed on
its chair of the sea, in symbols disguised as tilts, a vision disordered
	by spotlight, broken waters, loose in mortality, in despair,
CCC the dancing hull in upswing, blowing dark out
	infinity, that never snaps into its proper ring,
flights of depression, wandering past the spray, the tempest door,
	somewhere behind which is an abyss that never gets out.

·

Satyr alive on theft, a drip of it. I will have your job
dot, before I'm finished with my life. Eating the shopfloor
	up to its entelechies in backorders, drink the river
sluice for its poison, tearing apart the tree and wall, and blinking
	daily fluid outlook, beating on shadow, lost waiting
its turn, swivel and standby, its sexuality, its metrical
	gimmick grown endemic to desire, packed or blank.

·

Hakagawa grimaced in sympathy. *I only wanted*
he said but the sentence trailed off in the water, stars blinked on it.
	In silence we filed back to the waiting marina. I alighted
first as a twelve year old, then as a teenager, scrambling up and down
	the foldaway ladder, stood apart on the musical landing stage,
upright on the extant leg. What of the world that teems
	—where brooding Hypnos reigns—with dry dreams? I said

·

To the dark, unlistening water strung up in tufts in the sky,
pathic orange, and was not answered, and rain began to fall
	like rain, a loud mundane cadentia basizans ascending
down to the ear from the cheek upside Xiao Pac, stood on his head,
	and up to it on Capo Dot, off his. But this novel wet
would do, an answer is only so far, and as it flew and fell
	into the open car that took us back, we traded vows.

·

That is right. I heard the sound. I wanted to start out real
and could, *A soul hung up*, my adamant eyelashes filtering
    hot chicken fat distracted through a grate, alive, of sinew
and polystyrene screwed on to the seabed, in my chest
    that hole to tear our solitary breath out, fucked, defying
life for the world, perforated free to be my only
    filter for the fat, the grate, the seabed, one by one.

•

It was a situationist pastoral. In trembling how I tried
to buy Dot off with the pliers and oil and was declined, battered
    back into frame by the hot chicken bastard, blaming the hole on what
it tore out through to pin me to existence, where paralysis
    itself awakes my pains in thrilling strains to fierce desire.
But setting aside the reality of her decapitation Black Beauty
    and I ran anyhow hoof in leg to the Al-Rashid to score.

•

On the bill, headlining, UTN1, supported by the Fleshettes.
Lucas Manyane Fritzl owned the floor. I am the bar.
    The cold earth under it squandered just a tremor, my two fingers in
Xiao Pak, his ears in outer space, and space inside the void
    in the free, and everyone singing, anyone dancing, inside me
you are forever still, speck of catastrophe, white from the summons
    to live still forever, only you can, but as you will.

•4

_____with a carrot for my mother.
The time you ate the ashtray in Madrid. Primary care trust
    profit prolapse alias NHS the long way out,
what did the wet ash taste of, Westropp, cream, the sun in Spring?
    9500. We're off the boat and on the solid ground,
to stand for what is drained, stomaching *what* life for a living
    shoehorn you dig stupidly into water with, drowning

•

Slowly as the wind in wipers at the local Esso
carwash est percipi Dot retorts and the parts of a sky
    storm the *Bitter Pill*, trashing all kinds of expensive shit
stowed up in its broken middle, the split-level ski-slope,
    scored-in diameter of fingerlickin phendimetrazine,
as love will do, or loss will, if you let it; the waves that beat
    annihilation back will freeze: we'll drink the carnage neat.

1

To the anagrammatic Diotima I am a bare intuition of Vietstock. Do I borrow a more refined existence from objects that hover on the brink of nothing? How will I play out, if not worse? Frightened by this last ambiguity? Growing up insane? *Stress Position II*, a story that *runs up a blur of one metonym sprung from the dot idol into another* metonym sprung from it, like You You spreading his butterbeans and fruitflies on a hacksaw. Some definitions to start with. Truth first. It is the name we give to an account of events we believe in (but must we believe in events to believe in truth? If not, is belief grounded in indifference to belief?). Or else it is hens a thousand mile, fleshpot products of unknown origin piously recycled back into the diet chain, food fraud pure and simple. Finally it is out there, or only there. Now distance. Really, the distance is a square, when you look into it, an almost unthinkably fine square, and it will work just as well if left lucid as if left obscure, to a point. But when? You recognise the face in it as the one you had every day since you were a baby and the two you pulled every night long since. Why the confusion? Can you individually see anything? Can it individually be seen? Now a warning. You can loot all the animals from the zoo as often as you like, but you know you'll only harden Llewellyn Werner. You will learn from it as you never learned from it before, but in the end expensive wisdom is not enough, even for a shithead. The money runs out and in the end it's not there anymore. Therefore on the basis of this warning, in tribute to truth, looking to the distance, call it what? *Gristle to the chewy retina*, the head retina, back that name, or *How To Pick Up Thick Skins With Deep Pockets*, or back that name, or *eminent domain by gun*, or *men to bungy maiden in*, who are so nervously alive your heart will explode, wonder how to get on in them, or in on them, to be true by narrowly missing out on doing their identity like the *Push Around*, which you remember is gentlemen on ladies' left facing "Line Of Dance"

(LOD)[2,3] me[4]n'[5]s rig[6]ht hand in ladies' right hand at her right shoulder, men's left in ladies' left at men's belt, men's and ladies' foot pattern is the same except where reservations have been noted, anyhow you move around, and whereas *down* in this work may signify *in* or *back*, taken seriously, *down* must never again signify *in* or *back*, not even in a language given to inimitable pleasantry, or given over to it, when under the eventually superior pressure of being taken not at all seriously, as now? Which is easy enough to say, but to act. Alive yet. The dog gum Kievs 'in' the freezer 'under' the branding iron 'with' the dwell timer 'on' the disco ball 'over' the—I forget, anyhow they can *wait*, you have to tidy your room first. And when you do, you find life led as follows. In that distance that is a square we move around in an unshining white, light in the world does not resemble it. *Move Closer.* Our commission is to gather up nothing in handfuls, but I think of them when I say it as handfuls of grass. We do gather up the handfuls, moving around what in my translation of it is a maze as though she and I were blips. I can't explain to her why this is so terrible, though it is, because her blip is not disposed to countenance the thing in my language, even though it is as much her thing as mine. When do I say it? Now for example. And my own blip? It moves at the right point into the space, it is moved, except that would not be right, it is not a space; it is assembled there with the rest, and her blip is one of them; there is a sound, which it,

2 Or, respectively, on the days leading up to the above, "Level Of Detail", "Limit of Detection", "Loss Of Data", "So Not Fair", "Log Of Odds", "Legion of Doom", "Point In Time", "Low of Day", "Lateral Overflow Drain", "Quick Dump Rinser", "Last Order Date", "Line Of Duty", "Contractor Fiscal Year" or "Laparoscopic Ovarian Drilling", in that order.

3 « Celui qui entend nommer le chef qui le gouverne un grand politique, parce que chaque ligne qu'il publie est une imposture, veut être à son tour un grand politique, dans une sphère plus subalterne. » Pseudo-Hades, *Yes We Can* (Kronos on Sea, for-ever) [PAGE ?]

4 (LOD)[1,2] *me*

5 nce" (DOL) [1,2] *me*[3] n'

6 Dance" (DOT IDOL) [1,2] *me*[3] n'[4]s rig

the blip under my pressure, takes for a royal fanfare, roughly, knowing that it doesn't know where from; it is confused by not being confused by it; it is moved that we should recognise an event that no-one says is an enthronement; we do, but we can't, it just isn't that, the crowned face is just cramped together white-white and black-white, nothing like anything, a thing or un-lion; and the other thing that stewards us—just sound?— intimates *get back in*, meaning 'down' into the thing translated as a maze; and whatever happens, and it is always the same thing that happens, and happening is always the same thing, she is never hurt, not even when I am most completely scream- ing, because she seems—instead?—philosophical; and finally, the value of it is, that it is from longing to know all too well as I do how in that distance her blip ended at the assembly by seeming philosophical, that we grow up into persons who know what to call philosophy. Only you are not either blip in the end and you don't know what to call philosophy. Swivel both left, swivel both right, swivel both center, stomp right (weight on left). The shadow panda is strapped to the moon, your dreams are all juvenilia.

2

Go yellow in their inflexible burlesque of standard operating reflex. Don't confuse a *root* with a *bass note*. Following the poem means reading from two heads at once, each one pointed where it would be better off. But in practice you may find it easier that you don't mind. Two heads is not a difficult thing to take in, you can glance from one to the other, using the sockets for eyes, according to what the sex organs suspect is more impor- tant. *Stress Position* not in W.H. Smith? It will be.[7] In that dis- tance that is a square the scene cuts to a wedding. We are at the

7 I have looked in vain for an anchorage in the boundless sea of pleasure and in the depth of understanding; I have felt the almost irresistible power with which one pleasure reaches out its hand to the next; I have felt the sort of meretricious ecstasy that it is capable of producing.

wedding, which is not now a wedding but a reception, sitting at a folding table whose top is an octagon of grey plastic. The table is folded out horizontal. At the front we look to is a stage, and a relative on it is doing a speech that we do not give up listening to, so that only the back of our heads point at the current picture plane (elsewhere people are in knots). We hate her speech, oppose her, seethe during it, but it goes on, and because it does we are obliged to go on hating, as it continues the same until we will speak, but we will not be able to speak because we can't, it isn't speaking, it's an act, and in a sudden rush of choking and unstoppable loathing you are run to the front, which is not now a front but a floor, and it is because you cannot see what hands you have put on her throat that her strangling must appear not to be your only way out but better hers instead, as her face bulges, then it blushes, with every shred of your repugnance you split up unbearably scream at and press her, and as you are looking at this she begins to calm you, with a face very tender and unflickering in the way you like. Truth is beginning now. A circle of relatives is closed gently around us both, who stand in silence neither wanting to be recognised nor living not to be, at the wedding they are in the deepest part of the room, that is, *around* you, and her face continues to be exactly what it was, only there, tender and calm. *Her truth is whispered about her, not in sound, will you come open* and spill out hell in the papier-mâché mouth, not just sink to it,—and you are deputised to the answer that gives *yes*, in horror I do see, *yes*, these are my fists clenched and blooded in how you swallow them, why am I doing this to you, I'm freezing, and the sun light come in through the wall of windows is leant slowly across the very tender face just under yours, because all you will do is suffer for this forever, you don't have to, the memos are released and in any case redacted, the wedding is not yet ruined, will you not end instead, while you can?

3

Laughing and the white air bulging like a lost hair in the liquid. It fell out like this. The Seiler upright was made registrar of voters for San Diego County, subject to immediate *Brennschnitt* of its umbilical cord, which was *still* tied up at the Kitzingen workshop over in Solano, facing extradition to bathos. Of the much chattered about *Belastung durch Restrukturierungsmaßnahmen*, nothing but a gothic silence. It was after that that two sounds could be heard, distinguishable yet different. First, a kind of *tinkling*, that I in my rather jaded way took to be a *rondo* for the left hand, the black keys reserved for the middle finger. I with my long disentranced and offhand ears figured this was probably *allegro comodo*: deftly, in the oiled wards. We danced to this anyhow all night. We were cuddly in the wrong way, during our dance, like Barney the First Dog. Second, but earlier in the history of reverses, there followed a noise unfairly like *weeping*, that I in my somehow totally beat way took to be the message of the special woods, I mean the pure sounds of Kitzingen, highly flanged you understand and liberally compressed, but as lyrical as everything else in the world squared, and in a certain sense good. You laugh at this but Cuyahoga County dies for it, you *failure*. To this we would not dance, if we would. All bodies are either in motion or at rest, which is not to say—but which is to be *made* to say—that high organoleptical value is no guarantee of shelf life; and also that you're either shitting or you're dead, like that halcyon in the elevator with us that we laughed at, lovingly blind as we were to the *nachfragebedingte Arbeitslosigkeit* raging in Cuyahoga County for our wake, so that even the most erotic prestidigitation over the special woods catalogue will not make life once hygienic. You don't need a face lift to see that, but you do need a review of voting systems. Then we all had an amazing time. As if you also did.

4

_____ *with a carrot for my mother.* The end. Epilogue. So it was that this evening we begin with the end. What was the end? The end must be first of all what you are in. Introduction. Then when in the end you are a person trying, Introduction. So it was that when in the end you are a person trying to love, it must be by choice. But it must be by a choice you refused to make long enough ago. The end. That is, not by one you only just now refused to make, such as to know what that meant. Then when what that meant must be going on to the end, The end. Trying to be in the end like trying to love includes questions. But *these* questions? So it was. *Now?* And what did you ask them, The end. What what meant? What meant what? Or what what meant when what meant what, what that meant what meant, So what. So it was when in the end you did by choice refuse to choose by any end, Epilogue. So that that meant *these* questions. How can the conditions of any group's life *sum up* all the conditions of life in their most inhuman form, when the only group that qualifies for the arithmetic is disallowed the majority of pleasures? The end. If the thing I who am passionate can do most passionately is reverse, but passion is irreversible, is time contradictory? Epilogue. If you are alone entering the room and the pain is on the floor *only* because the floor doesn't fly away, is the only way up? Epilogue. What does torture really interpret, if not by the natural compliancy of pain? The end. Is murder ever free, and if not, is it a corollary of the gift? Introduction. Who most deeply put you up to life? The end. What happened when the beginning of the beginning was no longer the beginning of the beginning, but the beginning of the end, and what is happening for when that happens? Introduction. Did you ever once actually shut up so much your point disappeared? The end. But if I *eat* the entire contents of the zoo and am sick on him, *must* he harden? Epilogue. Quantifying speech is indivisible. True or false? Epilogue. Do the most frightening things actually stand for the boredom you would feel without them in a flash if you didn't already feel it more? Introduction. How does it feel to be penetrated from behind a mask thicker than us both? Epilogue. Who was it that once said that that once said is that no more *what*? Introduction. Two trucks explode today in a village east of Mosul, killing *x* people and injuring at least 3*x*. The whole channel reports it. Dozens of houses are flattened by the blasts. In Baghdad, car bombings today claim at least 16 lives, Press TV cite police as saying. There is no immediate statement of responsibility. The Associated Press say what was targeted at Shiite Muslim areas. Do you A? Epilogue. Under the hole is more frightening than the hole or less than it? Epilogue. What are the entire lyrics to the Meat Loaf songs used to torture prisoners at Abu Ghraib backwards? Introduction. Who do you symbolise most in this in innumerable ways right life? Introduction. Will having got there in the end mean less by the time you get there in the meaningless end? The end. Did you turn the tap off my love? Shut your eyes. Take any part of a sentence, like *this evanescence and lubricity of all objects, which lets them slip through our fingers when we clutch hardest*. Fix your image on it in a line, like *fists clenched in the spinning clay on a happy potter's wheel, the damp clay wobbling and creaming out between the callous fingers*. Shut them. Make pleasure. Get the pleasures high on a political object. Here there are many warnings to choose from. Know when. The political object opens. Read it. It is *a face flung through a jagged shattered windscreen like puked custard in a bin in yet another journalism photo of Iraq [a theatre near you]*. Keep them shut. There are three sentences in three lines. The triangle glows in the dark, shines from there. Rotated sixty degrees about the object tip it gives the instruction to pun: Kantian pyramid schematics, my little transcendental pension plan, a franchise to extort only your *petty* doubts about the real thing (in reality the real thing is the hard stuff). But the triangle was not always

262

that shape. It was bent into it in a fuckup. Review it. *Stress Position*, where the news *stays* the news. Who will review it? Somebody sing *I'm being very afraid*. I'm being very afraid that my brain is on the loose, trailing its vampire cuticles through the dust of our wasted fields, not untrue and not unkind, as the skeleton recovers its boner but can't go again yet because it's been stupidly thrown all over the place (note: rhyme cartilege with competitive advantage), looking for the fucking Varitemp cryostat through a square fucking chink in its own fucking optical window. The dusky backing screamers all do the *Streth Pothithun*, skidding across the disco on their knees. Change it? Then Ali says, punking you, Life is career suicide. Fail to Ali, shut up. Dream. Dear [a theatre near you] I just rose out of bed still tangled in a dream with an unusual and hurt feel, and since you were in it I thought it would be interesting to write to you and tell you what it was. That was a long time ago. Only a few scenes are now this side of meaning or able even to be summoned as flash imagery into my mind, though the others have left their atmosphere there. Other people lived there too, or would often be there. The one that's clearest was that I somehow knocked a grieving friend off a boat, a very slow-moving barge, its deck close to the surface of the canal, and had to jump into the dirty water to help him up. Again another phone, again not mine. The water was shallow, I could stand in it and it came up only to somewhere around the middle of my chest. It was a novel. The friend was someone I'd not seen since I was a teenager at school, someone who I know later joined the army, was discharged, had a couple of children outside a stable relationship, I know nothing else. So I reached down to the floor of the canal to grope for it. He was grieving in the dream because his elder brother had died. I felt helpful and surprised. The brother I remember had sometimes tormented him and more often simply ignored him in reality. I did that over and over, astonished that so many phones were at the bottom of the canal. My friend would joke about his brother's pornography hidden in the bathroom. You[8] were its author. Anyhow he seemed too heavy with grief to lift himself from the thick water, though it was his element, and it was heavy too, so I had to lift him myself back on to the deck of the barge. Immediately my fingers discovered a phone and lifted it out into the air. As I did that, my phone slipped overboard and into the water. Some of them were still working, others not. I now realise that makes no sense since I was standing in the water, but that's what the logic of the dream flowed to. I don't now remember the first sentence but I know that I did read it in the dream. It was not my phone. I went to look through my contacts. I groped again. There was again grief in the air as I turned the first pages and I think I spoke to you, I must have, though I don't remember what I said, but the grief was plain and you responded to it by suggesting, and I remember it felt very improbable and surprising, that I should come and live with you in an old house you were renting, and we could read there together. Everywhere I reached there was a phone. You were standing nearby. What could I have done that I didn't do with so many phones? It was a long sentence, disjointed, outside normal grammar, and all I can remember now is that the second clause was the single word "s". I tossed each of them on to the barge. It was SS. Spine Risotto, or Porn Sites ISO/TS 16949. Eventually I found one that I thought must be mine. I read the first paragraph. It was still working. The book won the prize it was entered for and was published. I think the dream then skipped to a different scene, and I was reading a book. I think I did know too that the book in my hands was more experimental and unusual than the one I knew by that title. The book I knew had been written as an entry into a competition. I never saw your[9] face in

8 You.
9 Your.

the dream, you[10] were only suggested by colours and your[11] exact name. It was called that and it was that book, I knew, and I knew or thought I'd read it before; but the text was unfamiliar to me. The word meant to me much what it means to you[12] in the phrase "Denn alles Fleisch es ist wie Gras", which is in Brahms. I remember now only the second sentence of it. It will quickly live and die, or will blow away in the wind if you[13] pull it from the ground and release it. I was surprised in the dream that you[14] were the author of the book, since I remembered reading it when I was young and not knowing you[15]. But then the tempo hippo turns *back* into the shadow panda, like soft skin into hard skin, and you're told that it's a cartoon called Auntie Heautontimorumenos, which may be a lie or may be a lie in verse. But then what may not be. But just then a human animal, just then alive, a latecomer to mortality, says But, kindly gritting his teeth and flossing his driveway, but in something like this universal tone of voice exactly, Immovable is this the poem end of the, What it allows do you to stop is right now, or, End this the poem of the immovable is, Stop what allows you to do it now is right, or it doesn't say everything like that but does it, so that in fact there are no options. For if there are no options, then there are no hot options, and if there are no hot options, then what? *And vice-versa* (and vice-versa). But Auntie Heautontimorumenos, how we plug her back in? Ali? Dead, in pieces: Hereunto A Minus Moot? I writ love as it was the mode to make it. I plunge my aching head into the bath water and confess to the foam. The foam aches too like fuck.

10

11

12

13

14

15

Stress Position III: The Answer

"Think but this, and all is mended"

I start with the superimposition of a gimmick on the Nasdaq HQ panic
bolts screwed in the fire door: pathema vérité, then stop?
     Yes. The first metaphor shines at internal communication.
A flickering eyelid says I am the concession to invisibility.
     Stress Position: the irreversibility canto. The foot is locked in,
the riveting other cheek is detained in the gastrointestinal tract,
          grace of circulation in a flesh of blocked-out fire.

                              •

     You can't put teeth-marks in a quasi-shin. Unidentified butterflies
fall on the motorway, scraping by like anorexic tendons,
          alligator clips on lactose, an easy life on hard drugs,
fuck with your head make voting look like knees on a shattered mirror,
          but so what who gives a fuck about butterflies, whitebait, plastic, ether,
waving their backstage pass about, priced out of your mind,
          saving the honourable inimitable general Anti-Thrust plate.

                              •

     What goes on in your head, or up but won't come down, I
walk into that bathroom a child and come out a black pyramid,
          reek of extorted ejaculate, c/o Cheney and Rumsfeld Inc.
trinken und trinken, why root out sensation in that blank?
     Fuck the linguistically innovative strippogrammatology
and its catcalls at inauthenticity, airing and drowning in equal parts,
          abandoning the ESX dinar to the jaws of Auerbach Grayson.

                              •

     Because the first metaphor is the deepest, for here it simply is,
but there is something deeper yet, formed into a skin above
          the string of plundered Afghan ears to stand in for the past,
where the simplicity of the first word in a flash is proxy to the last,
          whose percolated lightning stays burnt in. Who you are
is irrelevant or not is irrelevant. Nobody has to bear it
          or live as though it could be theirs to bear for ever more.

                              •

La guerre a donc perdu son charme, comme son utilité.
But the rules changed. Cosmeceutical disambiguation is death
    to stubborn expression lines, to unwarranted pigmentation,
the anti-oxidants that scourge their symbols to the brink,
    CAGE/NCAGE Code #: 31FPI for tender submissions.
Going in I saw how to come back. Turning, unable to cling
    to Philomel high on fire in a nest of empty shells.

•

She acts up like an emasculated Emu. Who will not screw
the sky back onto the bereft dorsal fin in the dream of falling:
    EHC gives KBR the FEED contract; the KBR
CEO at last gets shot of the Nigeria migraine; vivendum est
    Illic, ubi nulla; TSKJ teams up with N
LNG on the gas chilling; *Nachfolge* 'replaces' *Ersatz*;
    10 million man hours without a lost time incident.

•

The mass of the people heard its iron stamp. Why go on
the show in the first place if you're so bothered by the invasion
    of privacy? Too good for an obscure life? Breaking mitigates
belonging, which mitigates fantasy, which comes in universal
    credit pink and grey, recycling commons, peopling air,
why grope about screaming for a way out from that, if you listen
    forever the exit is extinguished one day at a time.

•

Count them down. The logic is an inner souvenir,
like the mouthfeel of democracy in 2003. The foot on the far
    pedal accelerates the coda, jump the line, scrambling out
of epic sanity, to find a way. Lucas: what do you call
    the moon. Hakagawa: the apparition of these faces
voided in compliance with the image. Dot: grow back.
    Do not waste the pressure this distortion still relieves.

•

Nine days in and as yet the confession hasn't torn out my mask.
The natives are getting derivative. Nothing will escape them.
   They adjust to it, as circles adjust to reform into the major
arc in a minor key, sentences become shorter, pick up
      a commuted tone. Back of the wainscot of regular friable ocean
pure thoughts on Fuzzy Felts. I want to get to a point where
      I don't have to do this all again from the beginning when I die.

                                   •

   That moment during a joke when you're pretending to be serious
and silent before you burst out in pre-emptive laughter.
   It's a social life, get one. Passion is downsized into
a clevis pin for epigrams: to err is human, to forgive
      beyond the reach of art. The echoing clock, the thunder
beating the glass, the howling wind, and, creepiest of all,
      the sound of steps coming slowly up the creaking stairs.

THE STATS ON INFINITY
2010

A door closer assembly for a household refrigerator of the type having a door frame with a front faced surface and a door having a confronting surface, the assembly including a hinge plate mounted on the door frame and having a pivot pin mounted on the hinge plate in a spaced relation to the front faced surface, a door plate mounted on the door and having an aperture spaced from the confronting surface of the door and a pivot post spaced from the aperture, the door plate being mounted on the hinge plate with the pivot pin aligned with the aperture, and an offset arm connected to the pivot post and biased by a spring in a door closing direction.

United States Patent 5027473

That from the murd'ring world's false love
Thy death may keep my soul alive.

Vaughan

THE PROXY INHUMANITY OF FORKLIFTS

In 1983, over 13,000 workers' compensation claims
to Erato I stutter this bloodless anathema
a veto on forklifts' trussed talons in face scrub,
tossed out of the world
of which you were actively sick,
waxing anaemic, brandishing fire-hose,
sick with anxiety but actually sick,
Borders in administration for recognitive aphrodisiac,
since I am shut and upwardly alive
a flesh that screws the fuck out of its bone,
count deep discounted stressballs
the Exploding Rat
the Ghost Cow eased in nice and
dark glut of idiot Ducklings, exudate from YouSqueeze
on the disimpacted grit slope to Asylum & Immigration Tribunals,
to yours it is to take and grip
rewinding the spoilers for Juárez, like this:
to lick at these reflections on the deep
fat whose unemptied extinguisher is
this blank life from routinely going out:
this blank life from routinely going out:
to rip its imprescriptible living strings out,
to bash this instrument to fuck you tune it,
rip its indestructible unique string out,
populate the data pool of ringfenced dead in on it
the ground truth pit sub specie aeternitatis,
idly ticking each head off
with commuter rail, to benefit
it lock to its pre-echo now restored to an inert
fact setting blank life from routinely going out:
this once to live a platelet's lust for blood
who gasping clotted grit out, I will die:
ejaculating the National Electronic Injury Surveillance System.

Like this. Tipped-up forklifts deflate off.
Noise of rattled finder. Lights.

      Reparameterized using second
      differences, sex acts
      as a time trend, equal across differences?
Frklft: Over the surface of that window are now copied
      blanks of effulgence on the late sky
      deeply not there there to kill my mouth,
      in silica and boron or their swivel vice of emptiness.
      Schmerzesgewalt, the teenage rind.
Frklft: There is in addition fire all over the methamphetamine,
      but it is this that fucks up its blockade,
      a sculpture of the executive neuron in shampoo made into
      the screw inside the ashtray on the men's room door
      behind whose point what animals despair
      like surplus mood, expropriated core,
      to clone the next life on the line, the charges unreversed.

      The forklift shifts on instinct forward just
      as much later you reverse into it,

acting the pallet minus sex lags of autocorrelations included,
the unincreasable isoareal pallet plunged in loss,
crossed in all the answerable love I have endured,
in answer for the genitals never entered, lit with
motion still unstinted of subornamental life,
that tender incantation it is madness to abandon
to be randomised in you, still promised for a motive to
make love immune to triviality,
severer now inside me, joked at there:
Live for the unnatural reason makes it unnatural in itself.
For *tlifk*? For *flitk*?

For underage sex on the propped up ceiling of the financial stress index?
To be stored out of reach, and in a stack,
eternal by switching off at the credits
reel of Eli Roth's *Darfur*, icing withered eggshell? But
once for when enough is for enough,
the upward cheekbone screams its mid art penance,
a summator to vanquish the signal isolator ± 0.02% span/°C,
and squandered love *Reductil*
spills in mud the sunk eyelid fritters like iceskates when,
as isolated incidents,
We last forever then, and no death sheds us,
running at the primary
run up a debt on living to desire,
desire to make me vomit fire GDP deflators into
19. If possible that dog eat
more than one time. If only
feed once, and eat reticulocytes, could be
indication better eat again. 19.
is possible
until *right now*, if not until *right now*, not any later,
until *right now*, if not until *right now*, or *right*
give me my desire
back or not at least what dust is mud,
or else desire
just hanging around
just lasting
scrounging in the maze
getting it
/
hunkering
down born free to be this old
pickled egg jar with screws and nails in and elastic and oil on it
last seen in the garage at Thatcham, cultural memory
smeary and gorgeous like Claude, shone

in its corner of the garage, playing its sex
games with humans, inanimate so oblivious
but violent in joy, estranged to last,
As the pallet I knew that to be wood remained interesting
hard wood
forever and so did nails I knew
that and so did nailing I knew that
for nothing, watching the earth turn beautiful,
actually beautiful,
but to draw conclusions from that
in wax all over the wall in a heap of rubble on the ground
like lipstick in a frying pan,
the forklift tore the T-wall half of wood down,
but its entire back catalogue of animals once having been done,
pored over, combed, picked through, redacted
there is nothing to be done but
be nothing to you,
as there is nothing to do
it for but to be doing nothing but
wanting to try to
live to drown the ice in vinegar,
wanting to try downloading *Amputeens*
to try wanting to instead of dying to *operating the cast* get *lead*
out *forklift* as *leg* fast *and* as *steam*
to you who are the distant love we dream
in sepia faces,
I knew that to be wood I must remain interesting
like a bill in an incinerated ringbinder
but to draw conclusions from that
always hacking up burnt ringbinders to get it
to let me pull it out
to drown the ice it licks in vinegar,
non-stop hacking up every incinerated ringbinder

burning to want to try to let me pull it
the bill I see it
look at Gulnaz
just hacking up the ringbinders you burn
not holding out for the one ringbinder that will not burn: the dark
indelible human pallet, unloaded now for rising,
seen to by the penetrating forklift,
says penetrate you break in on the air
lock stuck in your skin, into the vacancy in the stack,
the memory foam disaggregating warehouse,
trying to want to let me pull it out.
For the Israelis appropriate the Palestinian share of the Jordan,
and in the end become the way we are,
can't shut up, to open up instead:

-0.0.8 -0(.31+0.) in the short run, *Once*'' -0.5(0. (-0.
+0.29) in the epic to oblivion, 1985:
the off-the-shoulder straightjacket supplants the iron bib
and because we do, our lifestyle reverses:
The scratches turn into the lens.
And then if we don't, but defy the war?
But our spirits sunk in batches,
qualitative easing, brightly enamoured in estranged
feeling dispersed in erotic retail monotherapy,
the hedge blind outlasting the ditch blind, the amputated
blow on the amputated, idiot air
broadened like a mind of/into politics, cleared to billow
on common ground whose reset horizon
depends on what you say like pain on how a broken jaw,
moisturized in military shit storms
step changes pegged to forklifts dig in the bulging pick face
litigious angels gurn on legal high,
and go out the door normal hard-working people, and the

work is long in never being gone, like cinema
its burnt receipt waft up in ash over the warped ordinary
punched-in cash register, all inside your head
like sacrifice. In scowling wind, their ink unbled, quasi-gelatinous,
        death by expenses
        cruel and unusual
        an ordinary din
        to pimp no ride
        meaning entrapment
        come again
        payback for the future
dovetailed with the candied claws ordinarily stashed there, nostalgic for
the escalator *à venir, venire facias*
in purple wax and flaming pink felt tip,
delivered by the tooth stork in proxy for the flamingo,
no ordinary flamingo but its future precedent,
coming to stay for the weekend
how should you be able to be missed, present Flamingo
neither demi-diffident nor semi-ostentatious,
but who would be in discomfort,
and who would have scars, mucus, and a blood-knot blocking up
its or my screaming beak, wide open to equilateral
pyramids of,
First,
        that communication action produces value
        offers a clue for rethinking of classical labor theory,
        where goodness wants an equal change,
        to make sense of things between us.
        But the long-run price elasticities still outstretch us,
        as fat protects or harbours cancer cells.
        Fat as in low fat, local as in buy or get restless.
        11. If dog see you pick up his reticulocyte, will do
        the same forever. This called allelomimetic behavior.

Second,

A door closer assembly for a household refrigerator
of the type having a door
frame with a front faced surface and a door
having a confronting surface, the assembly
including a hinge plate mounted on the door
frame and having a pivot pin
mounted on the hinge plate in
a spaced relation to the front faced surface, a door
plate mounted on the door
and having an aperture spaced
from the confronting surface of the door
and a pivot post spaced
from the aperture, the door
plate being mounted on the hinge
plate with the pivot pin aligned
with the aperture, and an offset arm
connected to the pivot post and biased
by a spring in a door: never owned.

and Third, the dead; and of its defamatory specifications:

One shot at the end to find the one who shut my
head on love begun in one tongue first single atom by
single atom to take eternity two off work after an
incident three known as life suspected to be it
beneath a forklift sick at last of which if this is the
analysis is cast into a can four a tin if we release it
[one into the loss of nerve to find the thing who sings
its teeth the head they split in one meted out atom by
atom out five a one tin wrapped [in sheets of canned
shattered glass [blew around like candied me or you
six in a one can I was sick of this] incident seven sit
[beneath it I said that thing I am lost eight I am

bugged nine if [one a tin to make right noises in nor
be them state them eat them feed them ten not just
one as they are not for nothing eleven or being them
have them too the things] organised in sexual rings
they had out in a can if I made up my difference even
to death by the single [thing one in fancy dress as the
cross-section of a human molecule] scrawled in
bright wax crayon on torn ad section with [fire also
scrawled on it later deleted] in] one twelve a can so
long as if the death in me is impossible to put out and
to get out to me thirteen point six ent with forklift no
stop fourteen point] one if a tin but I ldn't fiftee po
[int four object won't] fifteen point six in principle if
fifteen point seve in principle don't look one point
one as how my point was already whatever it was for
so long as I was one] thing there at one life to
remember it being [but what it was in that case the
point of that [being different from nothing sixteen
point three I am out seventeen point eight eighteen
eate nineteen one [if uneaten] twenty [if left not
fucked enough twenty if [left not wanted enough one
[point four eight if a can on see that denied [me being
I] am fucked enough twenty two poi one four one if
[on account of my changed point] twenty three point
five in one] a tin] the point of change as [in the image
that is now] got out one sieve ironed flat is pressed
on is one fa traded to one one] [other traded to one
other what tongue slip through [it like water to wash
up in water to wash up in sparkling glue to the thing
nty four [point eight three the whole thing shut teeth
first minus melting a can and if I do it [then twenty
five point two seven as I do it now lost that a can in
time] for nothing to tin if] now as I do now and one
as I now [read this twenty six point six nothing] [I do

it now] and am the same] just as passionate [twenty seven point [seven nothing I do it now and am as good at not dreaming twenty eight point eight nothing one I do it now or am yet more good at it twenty nine point nine nothing one I do it now or am yet more than good at it thirty point nothing nothing one] one I do it now a tin or am yet more than more good at it thirty am one point not nothing tw I do it now a melting tin one or am yet more than yet more good at not dreaming thirty two] point nothing nothing three I do [a melting can [one tin or get at more than not dreaming thirty three] point nothing but not nothing four I do a tin melting or good] at yet more than its dreaming thirty four point nothing not nothing not five I do with a melting tin [the one holding your forever more lost face in my hands with your forever more lost mouth forever open if held open forever thirty by me five point nothing not nothing not six do it and gasping thirty one six point nothing not nothing not seven I do it and wanting to come in seven swerving down the hill on the trick nuts one wanting one if not desperate to be eight in me a tin will eat you nothing to be in me drag me around the cell the mall the security wall the perimeter of alsatian stressball ten the point to ten point in ten point liberated into a melting can one hundred and rty nine poi nine a tin point I nothing rip up as a point if I like nothing I open to infinity eyelids first one then forever the first you must back me as this into nothing else but a reason for love to survive yet inside a can locked to its burnt mouth pointing open. To infinity.

It is midnight.

A foul mist creeps between the droning trees,

Dries to a scab on holograms of bulging irides
In from the neighbouring governorate,
Come to see for themselves,
Inquirers into barcodes on sadly broken eggshells,
Irides fixed like doormats on psychotic pentangles,
Their black holes glisten in the diaspora of limelight
As whine the Al-Kifah wraiths,
And one by one the grim convenors count
Spotless deskilled skeletal slurs cut into toothpicks,
Spineless embeds fried on sniper's diazepam,
Tanked up preps all slurring their eat shits,
The rapid response post-avant errata of *Who's Who*,
pornographically licking shrinkwrap
Sententiae addicts, value-fodder for paeans to conceptual litanies,
    antimetastatic to infinity. Now it's forever 9.
18 am on a Friday, or an amphibious 6.
   1 % of the Wednesday before, or now is not a day at all,
but a stage set in an amniotic infomercial,
    where glossed lips pregelatinated in sepia scream in sips,
swap BICOM or *Now 74* for ode diction or grammatolatrous
    Varkala tat and highs, To infinity
stare out from my head down at the differential dead
    ornamenting Sunday
morning analysis flagships, foreigners in affairs,
seeing to the butchered Afghans of *The Sun* canteen freezer,
iconoclasts of the franchise of death, teeth grinding, pupils dilated,
cryptic barflies high on legal horseshit,
the boners of Gabon neatly rammed in part-time Lebanese
nostrilfuls of breakout at a time,
into my fuckhead finished youth not finished fucking with its infinity
but plotting a lock in at second base:
same shit, different war
unwaged by bourgeois dead who won't go on
with the dead of the C2DE demographic with nothing to prove but its chains

who ignore with indignation the dead of the Electronic Frontier Foundation
and Indymedia. Dead women,
meet the new necrophiliac new womanizers
it begins with fasciculations in the lower extremities
at a hostile acquisition anniversary piss-up in a graveyard
where for minutes you're requested not to sing that come to a lifetime's silence,
play musical chairs with the music turned down,
forklifts fuck like rabbits on meat hooks,
spilt on hot sand
and in the dead of night you do a sum
and in the morning deduct it from universalism.
Like chins off the chopping block, that's how we roll,
mouth by rote the entitled's subtitles,
make history poverty, inhuman love:

Forklift Fadeout.

But the unreheated heart is not soluble in dream its light
I burst to touch your disappearing skin
the kind I too am in
pulled over us
and got out of the car at the bottom of the dead sea
to rush up through deep salt
and scrubbed our mouths but the retarded bee stayed on,
we and the zombie bee,
but to draw conclusions from that
but to do what about it is stupid to do about it
to dream without acknowledging respite
but the retarded bee stayed on, not let among us; dichotomous
blood lost in the sclera frolics,
no-one will block it, what's ours is ours,
and the stun felt along it *is* democratic,
though not of the model lately attempted on Afghanistan,
replied the jack, *ours what?*

Light streams under the door when the milk falls out,
and though it isn't the door
revolving between the MOD and BAE systems,
it is the door light streams under
the door nothing chic, middlebrow weird.

REINDEER

It's late Spring, and the spiralling
sun leaves a glow across the thriving earth,
and eight million reindeer head north
loose through dark snow
to mate with eight million zombies on ecstasy
who will not eat you because they are not hungry
to mutter of old men's voices,
and we waste our smart bombs on the wedding carpet
like youth
because the people on it explode they become civilians
youths
mealy-mouthing casual meaty metaphors
you
humans who are secondary data like dentures in porn stars,
chronic reflex, arhythmia by rote,
the free vote on pathos detox,
and who will pay for it, and who will be admin,
and who will count
each word putting its connotation
out reindeer fly over the preposterous glistening ice
one step change forward, two for one,
in the pneugogic
conference call the musical
reindeer arranged in a mad ploy to rescue us
long fallen wide like the music of Skullfuck
young-old chestnuts in an infant's asbestos in the iPod
puree lashed on organic wafers
minim extremism is no longer the aporia of boredom
love is the bomb
fuck it eat the organ waivers
wake up you're making that noise again
like a dysphagic baby antelope chewing a penis meatball

in a drainpipe
in a Hollywood epigram
pearls and heels
two good verbs
looked like someone who looked like
the Natural Alternative Decorating Centre on Gloucester St
In what incarnation did she come,
or he, and when you made love from him
or her the answer to the problem
that there is no origin of bliss,
for you at least, and no definite happiness,
despite Wordsworth, and despite ample marijuana,
and despite the Wordsworthian high,
but that the not yet ersatz sky
nonetheless will not be emptiness but
will be made of love despite the love it's made of,
we are not there to make the perfect state
or here, but to defend ourselves
the new reindeer are permanently hungry
bolt to the high ground where the flies can't follow
and there are no crows or leaflets
or BNP or usury
in the strict arctic picked clean by sucking flies
run on the restricted endless tundra,
where one reindeer in particular
who may not be identified
but who may if he isn't
is the icon of a caduceus on the wet logo of China,
the icon of dust mites trailed to a Siren,
the icon of a cream dam, *Nil ardui est,*
until the same sun goes back down premeditatedly

premature in inoculation of vision,
and the oven door is shut like a butterfly
on unknown reindeer lips whose heated susurration
is an adroit kiss goodbye, basted
in cold blood from the unknown heart we wasted.

THE ODES TO TL61P
2013

And the situation is like that in certain games, in which all places on the board are supposed to be filled in accordance with certain rules, where at the end, blocked by certain spaces, you will be forced to leave more places empty than you could have or wanted to, unless you used some trick. There is, however, a certain procedure through which one can most easily fill the board.

Wake up my fellow citizens and middle class and go look into the mirror.

ODE TO TL61P 1

1.1

Each time you unscrew the head the truths burn out
and fly away above the stack of basements inundated
in aboriginal mucus, elevating the impeccable,
hereafter congenitally depilated Janine rescaled to a
grainy blank up on to the oblong top of the freezer
whose shut white lid unhinged at the back alone
preserves a pyramid of rigid meat, budget pizzas,
devirginated arctic rolls, only ever kidding in a
prophylactic void torn into great crates of glittering
eye shadow, dousing all its stickiness in dark empty
swerves, for no-one is the radius of everything we
are, a reinforced steel artery in the very integument
to be burst asunder, by reason of innately shattered
strobes as soon lived as burnt out, ramming an unplanned
crack into the door mechanism; who the fuck I am
now speaking to or at or for or not at this moment
is compensation for being completed into a circle
resigned to resume the first square, the first on the
entire board, and is listening there, afloat and spent yet
lost in streaks to the opening night whose primitively
explosive starlight is progressively nit-picked from a
lately impatient and fidgeting sky, not far too far or fast
too inquisitively squinted at its cartilage of crudely
lubed-up open access sex arcs scraped out piecemeal
and in single file, and once there inaudibly ask yourself
why; inside it is the fundamental sky of shining fact:
the abolition of capital is the social revolution: state

again this single fact, in too deep for any scar; in the end, which is right now, *looming* over a motto executed in the Ottoman style of the rococo circumlocution in liberal sex jargon recited by Ériphile at II.i.477-508, in the dreamiest mannequins' subsequent scan of which smudged erotic jottings allege to a scratched-out holographic ear the improbable lovable double-stranded far end of the primitive primary streak canal bound in stratified squamous epithelium to an alternatively screaming mouth, destined while dying inside to repeat before dying outside one last infinity of one-liners before snapping and giving up, or better yet pretending to, once you get it, once that is you really get it all, or not at all, directly into the hot squamocolumnar junction with its intestate teat cistern, a photocopy blurred into alienating aleatory *poésie concrète* by being roughly swiped back and forth over the scratched platen glass of the Canon MF8180C or Brother DCP-9045CDN all-in-one fax, printer and copier of the redacted catechism that stubs out the abrupt Shelley's 'Triumph of Life', later pruned to talking points, under the table propped up at right angles folded until they froth, to triple its unaccountability to an afflatus, doing as the banks just did not as the banks just said, I understand the hole that George is in, a dot whose innuendo comes too late, flush with spirit toilet-trained to life, but sucking on the aging raging hard-on held in trust for young dysphagia who only comes of age, yes exactly but at the same time, or at some other time like it, or at what is not a time but is still like it, if not exactly like it, or at what is exactly not a time and therefore not exactly like it, or not like this, or in an unsustainable combination of the above, to be waked to death and faked alive, for the known good of bored stiff rich men whose sexuality is literalised into a rampage of leverage and default swaps, hovering above minimum wage like a bloodthirsty erection over a fairground mirror, inspected from on icy high with seething and with licking, to want to absolutely spit it out, whose incessant re-entry is a background music *still* more popular than real because forever liable to be rewound, rammed again and again into the gaping ingrown unclipped ears of outgrown human sex toys gated off, ground down, caved in and blown up to do anything you can think you will do and then do what you think or fear you will do and then do as you fear you are told or would rather not do but nonetheless do or only die wishing you had already done or never had, grinding a fickle reality out, a kind of backlit soft porn nativity scene constructed out of versican, fudge icing and nail clippers, *shhh*, to prove the point of passion is immutable as fire strips (This is conducive to heat and does not require frequent cleaning, saving time and effort and money. Second, the pipe is a sheet metal processing products, the advantages of uniform thickness is unparalleled) or inimitable for money right up to the two-speed marital Martin Amis, repel all thought, one-speed once you know the ropes of growing insensitive, gaining the hill, from which a further speed is deducted for every emergent callous, until at the crux, when finally you give up ramming it because it has no point, it has minus a trillion preset speeds, shoots a mawkish moreish seed, basting shit and sugar-coating nil, whose real name is a liberal anagram for amniotic trim, not for TL61P or the reverse on principle to which the self-same letters cling in blanket terror of being peeled off by a rigid sexy acrylic fingernail later filed to oblivion through the eye of whose cameo done in grisly nitrocellulose and gritty ochre/lavender of your mother in the late style of the perpetually born yesterday Francis Bacon dissembling his tantrum to dead meat bunged in oil in an overhead Tefal Maxifry inanely overheated to open the end up half empty of Fair and Lovely a single, infinitesimal, silver plated, tiny ring slowly and invisibly spins, summoning in all the cast the obligation to remain within it, latterly as a cortège, our magic antennae screwed to our antic macramé, an opening in the opening night, savaged by the light it marginalises; but before anyone could actually get hard or wet or both at once for leading members of that cast, lead role models for our past, who beg to differ, slave to eat *the mess we inherited from the last* orgasm in government for sexy workers whipped to slurp the surplus spew of petty change remaindered when the banks have had their due, their in any case very eccentric final countdown redacted to a catchphrase for obsolescence per pro oral compliance with the takeover speculation boosting Autonomy Corp. 5.3% after better than estimated earnings forecasts at Oracle Corp., our flat back teeth drilled in the new international tax regime protologisms, refuting enamel, chipping in to Tesco, scorning accessibility, adrift in gum, virtual for real, adages on bandages, paper cuts in water damage, implants of the daily grind, children out the almost real and almost shut but not decisively shut yet and still shatterproof smeary and eternally not real window sing *the mess we inherited from the last* beginning scraps the missing past to recycle the joy it brings, the power set, of a subset, of a power set, of a sex power,

suburbanites of backstreet Überbollywood in flower
for the first time since you not only die
at all since how could you not; biting
starts too late, sucking is original,
is already there, free with age;
grab a plastic sheet full of milk to toss out the shut
door and catch it. TL61P infix and
feed the flame its sparks, to burn how it matters,
strict instruction voided blank
to prime the end for drying to a glare, bright
rivets on the profound water,
and under the water, the reason it's there.
von Feuer der Arbeit beleckt, to come
a random liquid tripwire, a head's tuft's caressed ash,
knotted to Iraqi satisfaction; by the fire
of labour, dead debt rips out prank alien loins,
this way up, to any moon you like;
the back of your first lover pressed in your groin.

    But if that will keep its grip
in there since not exhausted from
    without a light dissolves to rip
and shine again was all I am,
    plating the air humans exhale
in that window I flex in dark;

    to take the point not ready yet
to give you back but adamant
    by idiotic mantras to earn
the reason for love's apparent
    deterrence so long after you
my blood races I can't pull out;

you that will not come back led
in there to have the life you get
        too close; to be the slanting bed
too far away to make you up
        or lose you in; go under me
and stare at the same thing apart.

                    *

Our glaring end annuls in light
        what fire on the faded past
remains whose shadow cannot last
        as you burn away in bright

and widespread too ecstatic loss
        everywhere bends the eye
back on the slow infinity
        that blocks the love it fits across

just as rehoused at random love
        itself puts up its opposites
cut down to make the point it is
        not wasted in the end to prove.

In Mexico the problem has another dimension, owing
to the drug cartels and the human cost of their
iconicity, much of it dialectical and in women. There
they throw sackfulls of decapitated heads all over
the disco floor; just skidding on it like a male child
is naïve, but kicking them around is, if anything,
worse: at that point *everything* is deeply interfused,
even the congealed, invisible, virtual, abstract, spectral,
projected white blood cells rushing barely at trace
levels to the head of the slowest nail ever hammered

in Ichkeria into a pineapple, a wrist, silence, or into
the base of the hammer itself, a pat plastic simile for
a slapdash splintering spine, thinking cheap as dirt
and free as verse; Prometheus was a misogynist; its
testimony is the unbearable faintness of its odour in
your heart, this blood that is beginning everywhere;
but the present catastrophe (ll.485-6) rebrands Félix
Gallardo as the primary object, locked-up ladder
to its elite sublimities, so that strutting in golden
ringlets streaked with ashen highlights on the sexual
proscenium at the
boundary of significance we may know him, his too hot crotch
in knots of living weasel gut, whispering only just to love,
If it's not interesting to read then what's the point in doing it
or living as though you have to, defined by an obligation with
no fulfilment, lapsing to prognosis of a soap aisle?
I start my investigation here, taking my life in my hand.
Life rises to greet me, boasting its ardency in the carotid.

1.2

dusters wrapt in itching flame, streaked in limbic cloud
pt in itching *l* 6
blue sky on the setting water, nod til
made to still, remade in onward chains?
T
Looking out the plane window at the feather grass and spiders,
the three p bears
a triangle dunked in the oil prism a head left.
Who knows if what I'm thinking is this, or worse?
Dispersing the riot in smoke like love in conscience:
"the use value of a thing does not concern its seller as
such, but only its buyer." In which case use values are

exclusive to consumers, and consumers are in that case the Blinky, Pinky, Inky and Clyde of the way of despair squared, so that as our art is increasingly sold, and love is, and there are many more sellers, many of them good sellers, its use value as what the Nigerians call a supernumerary proportion of its total combined value including its exchange goes into improbable dramatic decline, like Chekhov. We *feel* this as consumers, not as one, readying ourselves not to, and are forever almost ready; staring at the alien in the thousand eyes it blinks, making up for consciousness with all the shit it thinks. Move your arms around, doing work. Click to the melody under your nails. Nothing changes this into a specimen of forever, very quickly, but quiet as impatience spreads down the shoulder into the thin end of the teeth the wind will brush the edge like water cracked apart, exposure for exhibitionist brains, plated with very heaven. AWM6140/3, allegations, water on the genitals, sisters in photographs, belt-tightening, electric dreams, speak in starts distractedly. The game has no ending – as long as the player keeps at least one life, he or she should be able to continue playing indefinitely. This is rendered impossible by a bug. You task Madiha Shenshel with cooking your breakfast (hawk eggs in fried milk, high in polycollaterals), then finishing it, then making it again (fuck, a dot), automatically spitting shells out; you prefer the boxes to the toys; Deborah's photo of herself crammed into her college wardrobe, ad infinitum; the hair on a thousand mothers; infinity ad nauseam; the internal level counter is stored in a single byte, and when it reaches 255 the subroutine causes this value to roll over to zero before drawing the fruit. This causes the routine to draw 256 fruits, or wish to, which corrupts the bottom half of the screen and the

whole right half of the maze with seemingly random
symbols, making it unwinnable. But reality is not at the
bottom of the abyss, the abyss is in time just reality
being itself, at least to begin with and at the same time
conclusively as if contracted – *soft* – to a single point
(a dot) at the end of the universe, when dark matter is a
distant memory subject for chastisement to the
fluctuations of military nostalgia (in her foot), and I am
not sure to go on, or how to, or even what name that is
any more, whoever you are I do *this* for, person *this*,
human *this*, *this* window for *this* crack, or even if I do
it, and probably I don't, the strings on a thousand dolls,
relief at Abu
Naji I cite its adaptation on bliss in memory,
retread via Danny Boy to the drool igloo, pseudo-TL61P
atom jus, disqualified for living
cleared – the fruits and intermissions would restart the
anaemia fade *this* the possibility *this* the price of bread
in 1792 *this* Mariana asleep in bed in a beansprout
bound in spattered marble, staring at the skin next to
your eye
free of that universe, mimetic of a smudged cherry
Traherne: love is deeper than at first it can be
thought, and the extra will last you
past care to a better joke about
you drilled through to infiltrate the gothic froth of Helmand.

1.3

But really to believe that necessity is exhausted, if it
comes, making haste to apologise for its premature
infantilism by a great, clumsy show of increase in
salivation flow, once best left alone not otherwise, by

going on longer, the point itself will still be around, is
a *joke*: embryo smut in the possible taste. Since once
you get from A to B, take your time returning. Isn't
it the problem that I *want* you to stare at me until
our eyes trade sockets, trailing visions, fucking our
mutual brains out all over the wrongest floor, not the
implication that hooding was banned in 1972 that asks
for an adaptation on bliss in memory? Light
sockets, the halo pinned to bodies in remorse,
devoured in a shadow life sends back?
Remember this: I sort through the boxes,
my first poems are there, the
drawings I made at school are
and my toys are, lead prodigies and barbarians,
Paints for them, tapes of my rock band
some vinyl of Tchaikovsky and Bach, the present
photographs of my first sexual lover,
whose face is staring with intent euphoria
and deepening tenderness at the face I
was, the eyes I shone in then, the light
in them blinds me now to nothing less
than under your caress I can do still,
and do still even right now, or very soon do
when I climb into bed with you and let
my arm shrink into your waking head,
or sleeping, however you are in there,
that room of objects and that room of you.

II

Construction may routinely be upgraded into life
as orphic vanity spreads backwards
its only motive for the present obscurity.

But deafness has an adverse impact on
interrogation, smiling at the lips in oil
for food is fast by proxy to an epic patronage
I want, take, scream, stick

•   •

You try to replenish the sounds that you hear
in your head, regimental amnesia –
I saw all the members of the multiple emulate me
unfold into an illicit epigram I now laterally hyperventilate,
one line with a joke end at the end
backing inspiration, breathing parerga of children and plangent dill;
ties it together, asks? *The Retracting,*
acting like ears, downed in void; a fur
of fire on *lick*
me you on this line when you don't
expect it when you do, this line.
It has a rim you take out to the bottom of the floor
big enough to remand your first genitals;
the rim is rectangular as any Seurat, to forever ruin
the way you wait, I'll be here forever.
A winding sheet of shining eyes, slammed to annihilation.

III

                              Nothing
we did could get him to open
the door the roof was coming down he's
driving us somewhere but where the
light fits like a door kicked in
the head on a shoestring right to do
its worst and make the best of you,
at the back to be alone
so that in the wet graphics spraying out the

spoils of the grave a dead friend in
shreds gladly climbs and with
growling stomach and powdered flower
roots to snort in dust steps on
the podium of odium to trill this elegy:
I have a dream of every man I ate in
all my life, / and after that
refreshment no zombie can pick his teeth,
/ but better learn to live with
what he's got and what he's not, /
and make both tolerances perfectible.
There's no way in as you defer to that,
this way back from rejecting it to see;
repeat yourself after me: repeat it
yourself after me: repeat yourself at me: I am
at alone in all the world a mirror
forfeit to beauty: the love I am is anything
what I live for, skin and looking at
you dead now but like at your breath still
sharp at the flesh of desiring we ran
out from, liquid across the floor
they tore down years ago, live in your hand
my face, a stick of empty fingertips.
The code TL61P belongs to a Hotpoint dryer.
You'll find out nothing if you look
it up through the sky in the screen, the vault
of exchangeable passion, Vertigo at
the horizon prostrate as an outstretched
cheek; but in the mouth that grows
in capacity behind that overflow,
Nobody can take away the word for it:
love, the provisional end until death;
TL61P its unconditional perfected shadow
opposite; Now go back to the start.

ODE TO TL61P 2

I

What the public hears from the police on TV is the voice of police management. Everyone who has a manager knows what that litotic brachylogy always sounds like. You learn in the end to pick out the buzzwords like hairs from a dessert you only think you don't want to eat now, whereas in truth it is what you have paid for in order that you can be too intimidated to complain about it or send it back, by way of sending yourself back instead, and though the mouthfeel is like a grease-filled crack except astonishingly ugly you study to roll your eyes, pucker as if embittered, and furtively smirk at the gelatine soufflé with the other patriotic bulimics. When during the live BBC News 24 footage of the clearance of Trafalgar Square on the 26th March 2011 the police "commander" (think of your area manager going by that name) explained for the benefit of sedulous licensees who own the perk of Freeview that the people presently adopted under the state truncheons are not protesters but criminals intent on chaos, not one because they cannot be but the other because they are, what he *meant* was 1. The plan to camp out in Trafalgar Square is tactically brilliant and must not succeed; real passion really does make disproportionate analogies powerful; the disproportion of Trafalgar to Tahrir would be no disincentive to solidarity; it would also appeal too much to overexercised Arabs, here and in the region; it would give Al-Jazeera an unwelcome brief commercial edge against Sky. 2. When the rank and file are angry and bored of tolerating teenage insubordination, you toss them some roughage of which they may boast that they feel entitled to it "after a tiring day"; you watch them get their revenge, you get an anal-sadistic bliss kick out of watching them do it only because you allow them to; they will think you are turning a blind eye to their excesses and be very flattered (this is what management *always* thinks). 3. It was late at night and the police in the square were being paid overtime; the bit of extra cash for its members would slow the impetus of the police union, which would be a welcome window of opportunity for the managers paid fortunes which are however already diminishing because of high inflation to dilate on our frontline cuts, in any case in spite of the rampant inflation of everything that is, owing to whatever is now the meaning for avarice, of which fit readers will be pleased to remember that Athenaeus colourfully remarked in his *Deipnosophistae* that it hopes to drag Pluto out of the bowels of the earth; 4. The windows at Millbank are not yet fixed. You are strangulatingly disentangled from the tiny body you barely knew would come at all, and pressed into a mucky adult clay you know will come every day, at the flick of your switch, whenever you want it. This is exactly the condition I used to avoid which I thought was impossible as poetry or anything that is the meaning I am desperate for yet now it is the only one that I make work hard; 5. Whatever manoeuvres in repression we fund in the short term will prove invaluable in the event of revolution; after the menacing from Blair Gibbs, the head of crime and justice at the Policy Exchange, who said, in response to the disclosure that police overtime payments went up by 29% between 2002 and 2006, that overtime payments have "spiralled out of control", we can suggest that the case for overtime is implicit in the need to be prepared in case the revolution should come at night; the clearance of the square is a practical demonstration of the inadvisability of imposing restrictions on overtime payments; 6. A modest spike in public fear would begin to compensate Rupert Murdoch for the embarrassment we caused him, right at the very sensitive moment when he and Jeremy Hunt were trying to consolidate his control of the British media, when it was revealed in the press that we had hushed up the phone hacking under Andy Coulson at the *News of the World*; a stimulus to petit bourgeois paranoia is best delivered at the eleventh hour, albeit at some inconvenience to the editorial staff, because the stimulus is naturally more potent the more convincingly the hooligans can be shown to have taken things too far and gone on too long, and in the case of a painstakingly slow containment operation still in progress when the news coverage ends for the night, they will have no choice but unarguably to have done just that; this is another natural basis for ringfencing overtime payments; 7. It will be an exquisite additional goad to Gaddafi and Mubarak to make them watch the police of their enemy doing with geometrical impunity what the police of Benghazi and Cairo weren't allowed to do; in some small measure it will help convince the Chinese that the pressure we exert on them in public over human rights really is just for the purposes of domestic political propaganda back home, which may yet lead to a thawing of relations between Vodafone and China Mobile; it sets a good example to the Irish, whose need for Spartan repressions in fulfilment of the terms of the loan we obliged them to accept from us could surely be made the basis for a new international market in police consultancy, right there on the ground in a bona fide tax haven; 8. Given the currently high profile of the Yvonne Fletcher murder, and in view of their being asked to dismantle a strategic analogy with what may as well be the Middle East as a whole, it may be possible for the clearance team to hallucinate that they are avenging the corps by truncheoning the Libyans; whether the team really does have that hallucination or not is arguably immaterial, since for our part it need not be true in order that we may enjoy the irony of imagining that it is, or laughing benevolently at the thought that the team might really be wrestling with spectral Libyans; the hooligans meanwhile can be allowed to achieve one part of their program, namely that they turn into spectral Libyans when you remind them of the repressibility of their *jouissance*. These meanings are not yet all equivalent, some do that better than others. If you stop and think about it, it might contribute to the pacification of the EDL, who can be expected to get a real kick out of seeing a bunch of pampered socialist Islamophiles compressed into a cameo of the herd which they obstinately refuse to acknowledge exists and runs politics, which may mean less budgetary nightmares for management colleagues in Luton. The meanings are not less articulated for ending up unnumbered. After all accumulation is about finally not remembering what meaning you are on, or not caring, but not caring turns out to be a treacherous attitude, best done on the sly, because all your care is radiant. Know your fucking enemy.

II

As sure as any air must spread the cost of any breathing
head thrilled out to cold perfection released from its
protection to keep our estimates so rough that each can
lean in close enough to bind on to the other free and
blind to her obscurity so every paralysis condemns to
cost analysis terminable or not the same live instrument
of breath and blame the high demand is prod the speck
to check its balance on the neck restructured not to
bend or turn or lose what might be saved to earn a
personal account of how in love with what it can't
allow either to be or disappear their average becomes
more dear loaded with phony fire to drown desire as
the blood slows down to last forever missing out as
mirrored in the late bailout or ever wash away the
smear of values else in sight too clear to stare in lucid
vanity transfixed to our insanity whose stalk is knotted
on a nail of sex smashed in too deep to fail or go for
just as long as wait or last a whole life wrong too late
but soft enough to trim the lips no kiss too infinitely
grips since sadly being shoved away is what makes
yesterday today disprove tomorrow shining more
robust than ever on the floor as managers are first to
know by shadowing the afterglow that blurs as
irrepressible desire or inaccessible is thrust hard at a
new mock dot whose proxy for the vacant cot assigned
its pun in Eliot is packed in silica crystals to desiccate
essentials for bare minds wintering in jars of skulls
bussed in from empty bars rebutting dusters in a fridge
not plugged in a dismantled bridge but switched on at the
wall and shut in protest at the power cut impatient
for pneumatic joy since emptying that girl or boy on
tips of absence getting hard to drink in yards of cooling

lard in envy of their hotter love of all our suffering above the Hotpoint *silex scintillans* the bright spark libertarians who lisp over the drone sublime get high on gore and moral rhyme and scheme on ideal felonies and bogart hash on balconies to level all disparities in passion only once as fuck so flashy bankers snore amok who split apart in bliss to ply the sexy shrapnel satisfy the universal appetite for more orgasmic natural right whose aspic and preservatives sustain neoconservatives to scavenge under god in blood and liberate his wavy flood Januzi UKHL 5 will keep the flagging law alive cement forever wet in dreams of Tigris' disemboguing streams of bonded revenue and dust shored up with picturesque disgust by poets mindfully concussed the more content the less unheard as vision sways its best when blurred suffice to say and get ignored like genitals too hard and bored for all the time you wait and break or mend to die will only make the memory of difficult passionate love still more occult and tender faces disappear as lost mist leaves a mirror clear to vanish yet permanently diminish not so passingly as love must in a slighted head shut up in dreams admired instead of shed like jobs to multiply the way out by the inward cry for fleecy care or finny drove or feather'd youth or all my love or scaly breed since with that shit Iraq in general must grit its icy core of heart and mind in not just spectral abstract rind but profit for the vested rim who mass produce the phantom limb rip open markets in despair mock cannibals who bite the air rinse spit and flush their sacred founts and whine about the body counts.

1.2

Still wringing the still obvious thing for side to side
hard pressed ears ring up inside sales in justice scales
by invoicing their vanished males in arabesques that
Sky regales or JP Morgan rigs to drip on Qtel for the
Gaza Strip when god in heaven trickles down relieving
Blair and turning brown the olive trees are burning
down the neck detached at no dispute the settlements
are absolute I ask a wreath fit on so hard the brain is
crushed like upstart lard deposited in spongy rats who
make our doctors bureaucrats mock children up as
innocents to prosper as their effluents and gnaw on
skulls in cellars stocked with shadows by the awed
and shocked.

Once Assyrian spivs, now votaries of natural election,
body odour clinging to the old regime, solicit for a pro
forma conscience in the sentimental porno form of an
eyeball rammed inward, to represent age; whether a
costly service when in lives or no less trenchant words,
a spent horizon dripping its limbs, parts and labour,
transacted to a cosmetic mouth embroidered with
intrinsic labia, silk teeth, outsourced love history or
cosmic dark, on the street whose massy brains lay
down to block the music drains, delivering the flood;
but what is vital and deep in me is escalated to a
surface for affixation to my sanity, reaching into a
deterrent void of mental shining after intertwisted
lights I press down on to mean your face is coming
back.

If meaning isn't obvious the brain gets mean and
envious. The revolution too bourgeois to come. An

always new but shut curtain, peeled by her single hand, behind which waits a face you wait to pull for being dead, is beautiful when shut by her double; it makes the window further away or not there at all so you definitely vanish in it. As by focus on what is apparent, art is dead labour too, all that can be done or said to end. Eat courtesy of nausea eight hours per day or longer. Go for Starbucks at Shenzhen on weekend. The very existence of a minimum wage is a very existent cage for my mum. Since I will not again be free to fall in absolutely or to delete or moderate desire for a touch whose sound is not to be believed but as dissembled to a cracking light, you are lost, stared at like distant fire through a screwed up eyelid, since that is what loss really is for Hutus and Israelis, the waxing ode indulged unto redundancy of ear; make the love that makes you disappear but at the same time instantly come back when kissing obliterated in bright agony to a grated shin or inimitable chewed-up spat-out shining spine, not desperate because alone, flooded with the only air required, shattering joy contradicts quantitative easing, replenishment of liquid life that punctually runs out, to bar us in temptation and to keep the flesh wrung dry; pure and fundamental to our blood sucked in sucked out and sucked off at RBS to fuel one man's innovative cost synergies you end up all spunked out ABN-AMRO minus LaSalle due diligence lite by lip sync, cuckolding Barclays, writing off 1.5 billion which could have gone into wells and malaria vaccines, no credit losses anywhere in the portfolio, the problem was the complexity of the products, asking what is your core equity tier one ratio on a lookthrough basis, as if to say, what the fuck are you not looking at or not through what at lumps of ice and tears is the contrite reply, shelled out from the eternal RBS reserves implicit in a trap sky of overweening negligence, while out the door the rest live past desire filing left to right, doing the cleaning and food, a plunging sky inside now too opaque to block, a sum too cryptic for the universe.

What the fuck are you on about the demilitarization of syntax? Anders Hoegstroem or whatever your concept is. An advert in amateur smoke trail calligraphy for a special edition of *The Sun* containing a photograph of a male cock ejaculating a human mouth incompatible with an organic face made to sag like what would to the averagely astutely cynical loss adjuster be hardly rotten if manifestly soaked floorboards in a style that is evidently senile but drilled in joy on every page 3, whose page count approximates infinity, all of them called 3, except for a solitary page, very close to the end, a mystery, a page called something else, a bonus page, an inextinguishable laminated palimpsest of the lot of them on which in an infant hand are artlessly scrawled in triangles the stupid words simplicity fuck and fire. What escape fuck are you on TL the demilitarization of syntax? Anders whatever 6 discharge your concept. A predictably instead of problematically predictably lovable adventure cage with no manifest theme for a domestic rat with a wire wheel pinned in it for it to run around in and translucent coloured plastic tubes pushed in it for it to slide down in a straight line or in a spiral and an opaque plastic ball in it that its child locks shut for it to run around in like a baby planet in a universe with no rat in it, representing the conscience of Lord Goldsmith. What fuck you, the demilitarization syntax bun escape? L1. Anders escape cape landscape, whatever concept. P. The colophon first significantly, then insignificantly, then neither significantly nor insignificantly omitted on the in any case long ago torn out opening page of Aeschylus's *Paedos in Speedos*. Fuck you, demilitarization. TL61P. * Tearing up the rule book just aestheticizes it into a vorticist collage of General Franks. You knew that from the instant you escaped; beautiful highbrow heel-dragging in unwaded war blood will not drown it. Go and fucking smash the world to bits. A branding exercise, thrashed out over a briefing document, excluded from the minutes. 6. The concept of a life is art, as well in the White House as if not. Sincere, tho' prudent; constant, yet resigned; but *not* in jail. General Franks will not to jail, however you collage him. Unoriginality is as old as the hill, and yet as insipidly venerable. Vomit the antidote, put the salad back barely touched, mute the flares, sand off the moisturizer, extricating what it may unconvincingly be pretended are incomprehensibly stubborn last globules still there after hardly the toughest rubbing fails with the glowing tips of safety pins, pick up every shred of rule book and diligently glue it back together, edge to edge.

III

Dance down the hill. We know for a fact that the tabloids are a protection racket for politicians, so we know that voting *is* extortion. Limp up the hill. But since the alternative, in any case not yet even on offer, is fully inflated politicians too big for rackets, bigger with wind than the distended dead end of an abdomen of the sugar-coated bloated Ethiop Aeolus, so that for the time being extortion it is. Both paralyses are best sublimated into an antisocial involuntary gag reflex at the least reference to anything but last resort, a dream in which you get to wish for things which you can't think you are told you never ought to wish for, gravely flagging up the hardly flapping haggard tongue. The natural ecumenism of the press complaints commission is on the face of it the nocturnal emission of the independent police complaints commission, nicely cold and wet; the otherwise eternal compassion of the independent for what is radiant, fresh kids smash up the porn shop scattering its bitty windows over the aisles of flatpack noumenal genitals, trashing shit love; the tax return of the independent police of the future. Outer space is deeply inanimate.

Happily eat the boiled hyenas but omit to suck dry their dark alarming skulls. Capitalism, the system for profit we all die under, is the infinite multiplication of values; the last resistance is sterility, but not the least. Queering war. Thousands of unshrinking eyes rush out a split open head in a prophetic geyser, stare back as wide and bright as the whole world, plunged in thunder over us, the ochre and lavender glow of the virginal streaking sun illogically scars their billion idiotic retinas. MAKE LESS, BE MORE.

Pope's descents to Beckett's dips, Keats astride a grave betimes, a Nigerian sex slave. A Nigerian sex slave plying its overstretched, hedged, oily ass at the dusty fringes of the *Biennale* to drunk sponsors of the European tents. Or what will not debase so much as shatter, or what will not rejoin but soon rip up, or rearrange with gratuitous violence, undo savagely primp or outright annihilate. Our amity is fitted for division. You won't say anything more radical than sex. But this irrepressible oral craving for the exciting controlled annihilation of values and invariably the long concomitant impatience at their boring slow debasement over the course of natural inflation over the course of things just going on not yet with the alacrity to be interminable makes the poet a predictable stupid rake, a programmed profligate courtier, his lyric on the fucking make, his infancy a mucked up fake, all ugly sex and textbook camaraderie and floor, and all the more derisory for sadly being poor.

The meaning of pornography when I am a child is that people really meant that, in that I would, and that I could join them, either by doing it for real later, or by doing it as a fantasy *right now* instead; coming with someone who would be real but not you in the future, or coming over you right now because you are not real. Intensity makes freedom an illusion: the present is irresistible; Reality is never worth the wait. The meaning when I am a child is the same one now. Intensity makes freedom an illusion; on one cover there was a childish sketch of a cock in my mother's hand. But under the other, my secret woman with the piercing mad hole; It is worth the wait. Because of this explicable hole in the end I speculated I'd get hard if ordered to stand hovering all night over tacks, while tethered to a pillar by the wrists in some vanished friend's mother's lounge to be inspected with explicit apathy from the sofa in the end as in reality I was, every night, in my mother's hand, and at last painfully pushed down by him into the bliss at the end of this fantasy, driving the tacks in after all that long agony to avoid it; because either you split me in two or fuck you. Do not leave me only whole.

Pigging out on leverage in Merrill Lynch is the new
Charles Olson. Flesh gets hard, sadly get used to it.
Without it you imperishably shine. Values have to be
fucking annihilated. It's not enough to do Pound in
indifferent voices wisecracking to your banker crony
about "the upjut of sperm" in a parody of an admission
of inferiority to see whose spontaneous pornography
can repudiate sex best, *quia pudendum est.* You at the
back, cremate me, quick. Resuming all your days and
splatter on the hallucinated mouth you sadly drool a
window on, yet throw it wide to let a breath sheer in;
once the breath is beautiful; The same old same old
up the you know what; Brief contact is not irritating
But prolonged contact, as with clothing wetted with
material, May cause defatting of skin or irritation, seen
as local redness with possible mild discomfort; The
oral suspension cannot hold the benzoates you only
dream: *Verfremdungseffekt* by arbitrary searches.
Lashed on thrashing fire inside like flashing flutes of
Gaviscon. I want to get rid of the squint, but how? How
to go numb from lisping in numbers? And how really,
not like that. If this is the way that this sentence
resorts to your head, why know otherwise? Where's
the oversight? Whose tribunal? By involuntary spasms
reality pushes you out, banging on the wall. There join
me Muses, in the songs of triumph, flying the friendly
skies, like this. What do you think of this bit, Bill?
Is it just a UPC for cramp, a one-liner about a crab
breathing white out? Blowing bubbles and popping
them with her claws, unconscionably erotic? Would
you first rip up then glue back together the words or the
letters? Why do you keep coming to me in dreams?
Climbing as if sideways back through the skew of
black and nothing like a midriff in your colour, not
dead for a change, not now abolished except in photos

that are also abolished, but living in the form of what
you are to me? I want a topical penis.
Excoriation of destiny is a cure for being impossible to empty,
a hoover bag in Sapphic drag, rehearsing our suction on dust.
In a closed circuit like mortality the last word is guaranteed;
it is by definition what you always get, that's the beauty of it.

Living stops to fit the empty
cap on your desire, right
    minded to allow the sight
to fade in blinded appetite.

Telling you again in level
voices to be stable for,
    unlistenable outside the door
to profit but to turn to shit.

So what are you waiting for
me for, the hot shrinkwrap
    disoriented in your lap,
once believed-in, only savage?

Fire comes on that won't go
out along the way you run, yet
    made to last for what you let
go past you, burns the eye alive.

But look at these caricatures,
numb by numbers, empty shells,
    new complexity doorbells,
jokes about what they are.

III

Whatever the point is, it's here to stay; and there's a lesson in that for us all, if we're not too proud to pretend there is. But in a flash we are only too proud. You ask yourself if you can be excused. In the future my ghosts will multiply the more people I know die, and my ghosts will multiply more quickly the more people I know die quickly, the SKU for everyone alive is EV-A, and the rate of multiplication will grow quicker until in the end the future is nothing but my ghosts, not even me; this is a comic poem, scatterbrained Iraqis. I would run words together like wall gashes strips, thinking I'd be right. But the outcome would not be, but something else just dumped on it instead. Years of my life wasted on war, depressed and miles away. *Je le vis.* The menu bar and buttons are displayed above the text fields: The line below shows many product codes; Use the menu bar to choose commands: In addition to the standard menus; File, Edit and View, there is also the: Dialog toolbar for fast access to frequently used commands in the toolbar can be activated and deactivated at the point View Toolbar. As for humanity, right now, it can be ignored or converted into a better problem – be degraded into a problem that was bound sooner or later to give rise to solutions like government, such as the present one. The public loves to be told that it has to learn to expect less, because everyone wants everyone else to have less, and everyone is willing to have less if that is the price for ensuring that everyone else but him has less. What a cunt.

The contemporary universe is strictly undersexed.
Same principle as the banking disaster,
one love used to leverage another,
one life more renamed the next.
Elastic shoulders imitate
the shimmer of no arc itself; screaming
Don't leave your unwanted love
over the floor and run away
where what you say is what you do
without including less of you, pay attention
the fire drill in the family quad at lunchtime
is not cancelled in the end. You know that because this is
the end, and it is not cancelled yet; I will
likely not ever meet anyone I love so much as
you again; but I want to try some men before I die.

1.3

The upside of the credit crunch is the defence review.
Think of it: the damage to Britain's military standing,
the 4 billion on Nimrods (O fret not after knowledge),
the limitation of the maximum enduring army force, no
more ratification by depleted uranium of the endless
moral ringing in the ears, having none of it, no new
material for the infinite ad campaign for the new
millionth Olympian, a pedalo of foam dropped on a
laughing amputee. You go downstairs to watch *Ladies
of Letters*, pumping the wound. And why not end it
there, courtesy of paranormal disgust? Look straight
in the eye, as under it you climb through that dream grated
in returning, livid end, far into the shape I
kept in order that I could love it too late later, my eyes hurt
in my heart, too much to stare at your gently dead face its
lips removing silence from the air they brightly shun

in an impenetrable hole full of conclusive human darkness.
My head does that, I am forced and even proud,
pulling you back to precision, to life by colour,
we're allowed because you're dead and I'm older,

   Shakespeare said love moderately
as mine as no-one ever was
      that line in "late Wieners"
impressing no-one, timing out.

   My own heart still beats hard
at the open door to know
      who will swallow it below
the meteor imprisoned in stars.

   Both routes out the window lead
to falling deaf to heavenly
      pretence but by flying only
too late into trust in deafness.

   Which makes it all the more real
but hard to beat, abiding in
      despair that love will not begin
when you do, but in everything.

ODE TO TL61P 3

1.1

Loss grows more absorbent as the swelling drains for good. Soft extinction beds down in a drone fit to repeat. But ripped an echo, rounded up to musical remorse. Floor as lids and wind for eyes, unsparingly not faced. Parting like a judgment with the sky, yet to come home. Agony lubricious as the Delta of Niger. Life retorts a triangle, the corners flare and boil. Inconsequence runs out and flows away like level rain. Fuck the waxes, shaves, implants, jerking, convulsions and sperm, real sex is the insatiable silence underneath. Nothing but the rest is ever whole; your distance isn't real or that unreal. Starting again is like failing to stop, the next fat lot of untold skin-deep trillions in derivatives, beloved surfaces bed in too deep to rip you off; The corporate thugs are conniving to stifle the state, to thwart its withering; the spirit thugs are conspiring to debase all of the currencies left; outside the upset junkie screams to tinnitate on empty air, prorumped in odes to plenitude not mine but sadly anyone's; the mind is what it is cracked up to be; these thoughts are not breathable, you are not ready to be breathed; the call sign, Carnage 27. Every time you blink you carbon trade, so don't blink, spit the lids out. You look out of whatever is the technical right name for the helicopter down on the swirling monochrome dust where in an unmistakable and completely distinct way a man is or three men are frantically waving his or their arms in a spectacle plainly intended as surrender; but during consultation with the military lawyer it emerges that enemy combatants cannot surrender to aircraft; you are in a tight corner; you squeeze the trigger and look watchfully at scraps of ripped-up human fucked at random into the dust. 80% and rising of hellfire missiles in Iraq were fired *after* the surge. Later, but there is no later, it will be obviously for the best, or have been, as a single dot is if weirdly craved as nothing in the universe but a single dot. Is this my work? This guess I will never be done with? Not the wage labour I do my best to ram my bed, dissolve my flesh, scratch my head, suck to climax and winnow my fingernails, contract my genitals and stay broadly sane in for money every day, or in truth not every day? The light of that day will slide in at the back of the window at first on a glassy outside but then in across intimate backs and through fronts and will evenly spread through the air, transparently retinal burn, the glimpse of renewal to token retarded despair, with the sun in your eyes.

ground to splitting air, the poor should live where they can afford to not where they are, redistributive justice; it became a country *full* of torture, omnivorous ravenous gut for riveting blood, rigid Muslim centrefolds, radical grievance pornography, there are some porn films in which a woman is only fucked in the ass, for anyone who cares. What she is insinuating you employ her to project is hard to specify; if anyone is listening, you do your best to get to the truth of it, but if nobody is listening then it seems less important to go for a truth that needs to be got to; after all you are not showing off; you can use the old one, what you really want is not to be the genitals fucking her ass, but to be her, to own the ass and be entitled to withdraw it; or it, open but entitled to be withdrawn; to be passive and open and plastic and traded in light; and because in the end virtual exploitation is for consenting adults less toxic than real, on condition that on principle you do not pay for it; and since in the end with every increment of market deregulation, nilpotent or not, the superannuated neoplatonism of that old distinction grows more and more scratchy and kitsch, until, which is to say, so that, its value comes back round again; so, the meaning to desire is that sexual excitement about the exploitation of women in pain is less deplorable the more unironically it can be extenuated by the collection of its conceptual debt to the always already widespread commodification of vicariousness and its outstretched rims of transgression, Enron to Xbox, either in this case and in general, the more widespread the more inviting, on top of whatever it also owes to the will to abjure the organ responsible for pain, as also in its turn for love, in this case and in general.

1.2

Reactionaries think life should mean life. You don't believe in rehabilitation. Everyone is alone when she orgasms, caressed into an empty word. On screen during my existence, and in the last analysis in lieu of it, a really beautiful woman is explaining that Britain must be prepared to fight to retain Thatcher's European budget rebate. *Selah.* Giddy detestation of senior liquidity managers, strong aversion to strategy consultants, deep disgust at lead auditors, growing impatience with industry relations directors, spasmodic shrinking from financial modellers, rational fear of property loss adjusters, slight suspicion of corporate accountants, psychedelic distrust of branch compliance officers, agitated antipathy for growth managers, ancient nausea at contract administrators, dinky distaste for equities client service heads, labile abomination of senior enterprise application architects, melodramatic dread of heads of international payments, cute dismay over dispute consulting vice presidents, cocky chagrin at directors of pricing strategy, wholesome horror of reporting and valuations accountants, inevitable irritation with fund controllers, mawkish mortification by renewables project finance associates, happy hostility to high yield analysts, untakeable misgivings over multi-billion dollar special situation fund junior analysts, smart dislike of debt finance associates, rambunctious loathing of fertilizer traders, shitty animosity for corporate finance generalists, implacable deprecation of fund placement relationship managers, depressed estimation of equity derivative confirmation drafters, blind rage at trainee futures traders, greasy disapproval of sell side analysts, imperative repugnance at flow rates desk strategists, sclerotic conflict over front office generalists, unschooled coolness on arbitrage traders, fussy disfavour of clearing margin managers, bent enmity with solutions specialists, elegant spurning of heads of securities, fevered shuddering at exotic rates associates, being discombobulated by top tier attorneys, attitudinistic trashing of prime brokerage associates, involuntary flinching from algorithmic traders, iffy qualms with quant developers, instant revulsion at options data analysts, hard-won hang-ups about life and health actuaries, automatic melancholy when confronted with corporate actions specialists, nuclear abhorrence of continuity managers, petty incredulity at transitions co-ordinators, complex disaffection for performance improvement operations professionals, real hatred of transformation managers, waning displeasure at heads of decision support, discreet pique at heads of client integration, evangelical vexation at asset servicing specialists, irresponsible annoyance about transfer agency operations managers, fruitless fretfulness over distressed debt fund analysts, mealymouthed misdoubt of credit sanctioners, overdue animus for debt markets writers, harrowed disbelief at credit partners, plangent repudiation of restructuring reporters, gruelling denial of structured credit surveillance analysts, necrotic mockery of assurance managers and irremediable illness of disposition toward regulatory affairs consultants getting social housing down to the last unfuckable man means that you don't really want the communism you say you want. For only something has to change and fast. You can't love everyone because you can't do all the billions of different types of love. Do the wrong one and you'll never forget it.

Since not a single song I made is comprehensible to you, I think I must be too bourgeois or indigent to praise you. One song that was never sung you archived for me in the breast, unlistenable outside it, meant strictly for consolation, when as the inconvenienced heart is turned off and the world erased it scruples on its part in peace not squandered but in heaven.

it is a good ear and it has been licked allegedly hard but it will not fly in payment for the annealed ultimate fragment of empty fridge or vagrant spigot to ultimately glut on later sublimed into a loss leader whose collateral loss is implicitly infinite, in instalments, for in your defence it turns out the whole kitchen was always and on purpose roughly this unsalable,

whatever sort of incredibly weird noise it mutes in peace
signs
/
lost to how I matter, ignorant of the youth of paradise
the hummingbird cell, machine guns everywhere
you look. AQI actually using mentally handicapped
persons to attack coalition forces. They used exploding
women from the attic. Poetry evolves from a vivid
play of nerves and confusions into sedative aporiae in
mock-heroic marginalese, if you don't take precautions
to prevent it. Maturity is learning not to flinch at childish
swipes and kicks, to know when harm is seriously
meant. The really beautiful woman who is yet to explain
how I should fight to retain Thatcher's rebate is now
bent over into a suggestion about how to prop up the
euro; I can see into her womb.

*

It's dark in there, Deborah. Whatever I am doing
now, it gets a part in there; I cannot see why else I am
not here. The void is to my left and not in front of
you at last. In the future, which is the front for too
late, there will be a virtualalium where you call up
everything left in the entrance; everything I am was lit by
love, but is now independently bright, on account of being
perceptible as it is; social justice prevents adequate
concentrations of capital. When you get older, genitals
grow less interesting; spited, the integral glass
forever fades into its shattering finish, dictating erotic percussion,
as love no less appears to end
but nothing can retard that turn
as fear that it will disappear
like antiseptic on a burn
to speak for the rampant Polish doing our dead end jobs in bed

by dreaming of us; but the reason it's that
way is what will keep it that way, to own pleasure unthinking,
to live another day and kill the rest, a skimmed-off sky on fire
unpractised in desire to stay put.

Death please spare me over for another year, your life
depends on the favors of man. But he turned out
to be a sex slave. That was how class boomed before
everyone subverted the theoretical structure of it.
Imagine whatever you think is affordable housing,
now imagine why anyone should get it. I'm never scared
to be alone any more, but I will never give up; just as
a tragedy is something you are obliged to imagine must
be capable of teaching you something, and a comedy
is something you are not obliged to imagine must be
capable of teaching you anything, so you are not
obliged to imagine you keep just knowing this, taking
it, making it up, or doing nothing, least of all for a living;
all the times you came from what I did in a row make an
alternative eternal life feel possible not as stand-up but
in fact; just as, so that those now abandoned moments
of joy can have a supplement in the form of cavities
that you can't stop playing with, holes for your most
private microvilli, the damages are temporary because
they seem so forever, by convincing you that they
always do. What it feels like is a game, one where you get
life after life; but though you go back to the beginning
whenever you want and make it more auspicious by
knowing what you have to do on the later levels, you
never get to what the German philosopher G. Dubya
Hegel in a pleasingly more hyperprolactinemic
connection once called *das Unwankende*, a word also
used in Nietzsche in connection with Apollo on the
pretext of his inflexible detumescence.

The same shortfall would later be the spoilt brain child of the wife of King Yorgo of Greece, in her hypnopompic pseudohallucination on the surgical countertransference of her own clitoris and its ego; one of the Napoleons will do a sponsored spin in his shallow grave of scrambled dolphin egg, one-way mirrors, for every explicit dousing in caustic of the Romantic subject on flexitime you do in an uproariously automated language game incontinent of its only concept and contemporaneously versified with stylishly conscious if not on that account deliberate ineptitude in order to be eulogised at symbolic profit as the *last* last farce of the authentic middle class subject in America, to boost property values in its most desirable urban centres, the flagging flagship flarf salons of New York universalism.

if that is what it takes, to live by blunting futility; we look at each other's parts under the table, Jackie and I, hiding our eyes in the heads we come with, so as by the beautiful misidentification of excitement with fear to remain children forever, a proof of endurance that entitles us to be only now for the first time disconnected from one another, anywhere on earth; I don't know who she is or what she amounted to, I haven't seen her since then; she may be tied up in a Fallujah basement in nothing but a hood, toe-separators and a face dildo; but whatever she is thrilled by now, and whatever she lives in fear of, I trust in truth that somewhere beneath all the real objects there still shines to her distraction the first image of the male genitals I gave her, wrongly flickering, spitting blanks, preserved in trailing clouds, tiny and perfect, the origin and corner of my love. I am also charmed with many points of the Turkish law, to our shame be it spoken, better designed and executed than ours; particularly, the punishment of convicted liars: they are burnt in the forehead with a hot iron, being proved the authors of any notorious falsehood. I should go on to tell you many other parts of justice, but I must send for my midwife. If you read Marx when you're stoned, it sounds like Beckett: "Grace to be born and live as variously as possible."

*

All three parties whipped their members. Invisibility spreads up from the hand into the arm and shoulder, so that the economy resembles an archaic torso whose python is thus at liberty to ingurgitate its lyre; love is very childish to the point of no return; there is, merely there must be, in the universe a planet identical to the one you are on, but for the solitary adjustment that the person who is you on it now and who was already you on it when you were still here on this, and who will be you here on this when at last you are there on it, if you are, has never once agreed to indecipherably blur, not for a second there, or less, into anything that is worth being merely about you, nor ever once asked if you are here, now, on this, are you there, or what you are here on this for if you are, or why you are not yet on that like he is, and doesn't drink like you do here, or smoke so much drugs, and for such a good reason that the mere rumour of its existence is a light whose dimmer is natural broken, that neither of you get. Rummage while adrift, fixate when you get back. That's the epic of thought, recollected by memory like an apron string; TL61P sentimentally hacked into the bark with a sterilised syringe full of futures and eggshells. How do you reconcile wanting to be as big as possible (within credible anatomical limits) with the indisputable reality that you were very small in the beginning, where love was primary and not pegged to the dollar or spoiled by being a replacement, except by adamantly filling up a beloved person until it hurts rather than barely impinging on her in embarrassment like a spongy earplug rested on a cross-section of mushy pea? I put Christian in my mouth under the blanket, played with him as if gargling. I didn't know what to do, so it felt better, authentically childish. I had to sleep in his bed because my mother put me there, as if killing our father; I could hear her sobbing downstairs at being stood up but not listen to it. Later that night I had to have been asleep. He asked later that we keep it secret, once we had learned that you can do that. I was fine with that, though I also felt that it was somehow melancholy that such a simple act of pleasure between people still roughly equal at that age should need to be made into a source of fear, when all we had to fear was other people, who could surely be imagined to come under the same blanket; I wanted everybody to get something out of my mouth. What comes from it now is this ode, bright abolition to apathogenesis; I stare at the white screen wanting to know what comes of it next, or later; and whether I am living or dead depends on you, and when you read it; it depends who you are, like tides on the moon, blood on the measured heart.

1.3

Dying will not mean wasting your life but bearing to pass for nothing. It means not waiting for life to bear in the past for nothing else. Whatever is nothing but next to come, bearing is intrinsic. You learn it inside out then disappear, or are probably outside already. But how is outside when the difference sets to bear the nothing there. The point is not to unlearn love, try to love nothing. It stops too strictly infinite: attrition must be sung fuck that: each and every loss of it will mean the edge away: mean your life but nothing else, love for nothing gets it true. Passion must be learned back start to end infinitely or your life will end without you.

> The ratings cut to junk PDD-NOS ratings triiodothyronine parts shortages, it shall be you lashed naked short; a tight borrow fire engineering Lehman pre-junk libidinous prongs, solid waste TDO PID 6 ratings go gloat fit to fringe;
and once more to live and grow
    as one by what we never give
enough of any life for, but
    rejoin us by refusing love

to memory will fake and spin
    apart synthetic as smashed in
more readily is hard to prove,
    the answer is not right needed.

As on the missed and single way
    refusal is its own reward,
my best of you who are of me,
    and minded its eternity.

Drag her off the sofa and up the stairs. I do want to hear that, I do want its reimbursement, I don't want to ignore how it also says what I don't; but you begin to know that the iron *would rather* be left on, acting on a blind impulse to claw back *anything* to fetishize; until finally, the flow of that progress is now and then more or less imperceptibly interrupted by a bucket of sand, bunking off a work-song on the bourgeois bogus fringe. Your mother's tongue a prod of junk, her chin in a flying cowpat. What do you mean as if you are beautiful? I mean as if you never disappear. Will it equally prove nothing? I can still imagine what it would be like to see your face moving about and breathing, breaking open with laughter, a harmless shadow on your neck, taking your drugs with me, then mine, floating in the bathroom; you grow up as a flower in my head; you had a moderately big ass; you wrote pretty surrealist pornography about your love to me; I could at least pretend to be able to say anything to you, and believe in what I knew was the pretence while it lasted by not credibly acknowledging it, and you could do the same for me; but now you're gone, and I'm the government. But really you're just away. The music of the ice cream van is scrunching up the hill of tar, don't be ordinarily afraid; liberals want the state to be a way of life. But we suffered as a society from being too optimistic, we thought the good times would last forever. That led to the de facto socialization of credit, rather than what I wanted at the time, and still want now, and may yet definitely want forever, the planned socialization of labour, so that the payout of immiseration wound up infinitely deferred. That mistaken epic of bad socialization is the material base for the late deconstructive superstructure, a mind impressing limits nicely warped but going flat. The rest of us, if you can believe that, are best abandoned to trade our way through clinical depression in infamous cycles on that fat roundabout with the mat. Think of the things you bring home and cram into your house, and all still there. What rips apart the ironed sheet to find its messy face asleep, dreaming of the Congolese reserves. But the private sector will

take up the slack, by genustupration of the levers of
fiscal power that operate the rack, taking up the blessed
strain of ownership from Iraq: unemployment will
come stretching down. Mahler is beautiful for being as
if infinitely resourceful in a climax; you want him for
a meaning of his life. Bush gave evil a bad name. It's
like you're still living in 1990, thinking you can have
everything you want.

ODE TO TL61P 4

1.1

They brought *rapists* in to break the strike. Labour are looking for symbolic targets to cause symbolic political discomfort to the banks. As you get older, you learn how to find older people attractive; sexuality is adaptive but love is intransigent.

*

Obama wants to cleanse the US senate of filibustering. Elsewhere the secretly mendicant unknown of Nigeriana Director & Senior Executive Officer Peter T. S. Wong alerts millions of perfect strangers, "we have decided that I will have you claim this." This information is repeated until the meaning of elsewhere comprehends it and won't let go.

*

Fit your life on what you want, not as you abjure. Nothing is so *had* as us, the roller floor of ruled-out flesh, spun but to the cheapest blur; dusting out the only once, never again sharpest corners of mental lust again, snapping at the nail that feeds it, staring into bed time. Attend to how that bad tone evens out.

*

What can't go on forever, show me how: the answer is

rolled out in other lines; the fish made for the
fairground can't allow: the reason for its point is like a
cone; asking what in the flicker under that: which you
may wince to call your curvature; can be lifted,
is laid flat: the sexual soul perverted for its cure.

*

There was as fine a row of boys and girls as you ever
saw; some beautiful faces, and one exquisite mouth. I
said I would kiss Louise, a beauty I knew frightened
me, because, if I can't escape taking it too deeply by
kissing her, in the, I now say, approximate portico in
concrete I knew opposite a wire fence threaded at
random but distractedly with abstractions of childish
plants and weed, after school; because I felt we had made
a contract that must be broken to seem premature;
that neither of us would go through with it; I am in
that room waiting as if desperately for the lesson
to end; it does and we both run to what we knew;
I ran away. I never got to love Louise. I did not kiss
Louise. Later I would love to have sucked her vagina.

*

Mother, when you were fucked you sang badly. Now
you sing fine, never to be heard.

*

It can't be done unless you fail it too. I wanted the
clouds to make it *impossible* to get down, not to be able to
see *anything* on the floor, to be stuck up there with you
in that freak weather forever; and do I not want the
same thing now, only with a different person and no

alternative precipice? There is no irony in that, it's a truth about excitement; money in the dark blue vault, the sanity of stars.

*

I'm going to *kill* the neighbours. That thumping in the walls. They'd better be having a *fucking good* time.

*

The beautiful thing about you is more than anything everything in the world I still love to do. There is a competitive advantage in remaining to be done; when I first thought them, none of these meanings was paralysed. They run and run. You are infinitely disadvantaged by persisting to the past. A dream / I dreamed you long ago, now again begun.

*

TL61P is a piece of shit – an infinitesimal piece. You barely notice it come out. You wouldn't know you're doing it, but lost behind your back. You could fit trillions of them into a rat shit, these asset values for which no vesicle is too commodious. Fuck me vapid. Professional advice to aspiring writers is often to write only the catchy first few sentences or the paragraph that really drags you in, and send that in, because your best bet is agents will give you a contract on the strength of your having attention grabbed. Your song is in the gaping booth, the ballot slip your lyre, whose missing strings attached in truth are tuned as you alone require. Over time the investment of writing in politics dries up, so that fascination in the spin cycle can be made redundant; look at Yeats. Versification burned out one layoff after another. Solemnly inhume the car keys, Apollo is randomly fucked; TL61P is a shower of lube in powdered milk: but it is an infinity too.

*

Powdered shit. Blow out the candles. Socialise the risk.

*

You can pick up social history by watching the more ambitious documentaries about the tours of Black Sabbath (careful with this).

*

I am in you like I am in my skin. Except that you burn in me.

*

The anti-war movement was too eclectic, as celebrated by the transparently liberal media; the pensioners and teenagers let down the Muslims and the SWP. There was not a basis in natural sympathy, but recreation around a core of disgust; you find the same problem for art, whose ongoing reception fades into an endless praeludium to the absolute banalisation of sacrilege. I stood on the plinth of the statue and looked at the crowd, and out over the park, at the enormous stream of people that I would make into my people, genuinely from the best motive, I was ill, and I thought that it was so large that with some intelligent coordination it could take over the city of London by passion, seizing the telephone exchange and the garrison and the armory, like Trotsky, whose portrait is now in my bedroom on top of the 1715 edition of the *Fairy Queen*, whose subscribers included the Surveyor General of the Ordnance; that's how fiction operates, magical patina all the way down; it was a threat to the state, but the state was too big; it might have worked in the Congo.

*

I keep meaning to live to the end, but you have to go on without it. After the days of rage we felt isolated and marginal, in concert with the third world uprisings. Bling your war home. The underground is all inside your head.

*

I do not blush like Pliny at our miserable origin. Face is a verb for retard; silence the verb for acquit. The fuzz box clams up stage by stage, Mount Rydal to Under Mogadishu: the point is to become transparent enough to calculate your way to the rim.

*

You see through love, and that deludes your sight.

*

Run at the end and drop the open mouth. The Sales Manager at ABC Tampa drooling over the 15 million in Romney ads is your too-busy-being-productive-to-be-incestuous father, who is decommissioned into poems mocking *Facebook* by *Facebook* generation poets

clinically dependent on *Facebook* for their unfolding
sexual self-identification, whose itchy-disgusted-wilful-
compulsive-minor-thrill-seeking in the deflective
surfaces of an anti-social real-time on-screen diagram
of diminishing human returns is also but as it were
only collaterally the hottest wellspring of capitalist
evolution, chivvying love into the form reserved in
psychological experience for the successful circulation
of blood values whose origin in elective data entry is
no reflection on their climax in the predicted hundred
billion dollar flotation.

*

Mitch McConnell wants to clear out the filibustering.
A love song to the death of intimation, the eye in flower
darkness rips its shadows in
to hide the flood of unimagined ends, the unspeakable,
unendurably too unstoppable, unthinkable human orgasm.
How perfect have been all those I have given.
How many have been all the ends I taught.

*

Make it now. They hate our way of life.

*

The coinage of paedophilia is attributed by the OED
to Havelock Ellis, who in his *Studies in the psychology
of sex* (whose first volume begins with a study in the
evolution of modesty) classified the sexual love of
postpubescent individuals for prepubescent individuals
as an "abnormality". We embraced a new ideologeme.
Since those first beginnings in what innumerable

psychoanalytical thinkers confined to the humanities can now conceptualise as the "pathologization" of too durable infant desire, keeping up childhood for too long, our machinery of classification has been melodiously refined. Besides paedophilia, which now means the sexual love of prepubescent individuals in particular, we now have hebephilia, a diagnosis for the sexual love of individuals in the early stages of puberty, but not earlier; ephebophilia, a diagnosis for the sexual love of individuals lately progressed out of puberty (these last two are sometimes also called korophilia and parthenophilia); teleiophilia, a diagnosis for the sexual love of adult individuals, whom we mirror; and gerontophilia or graeophilia, a diagnosis for the sexual love of elderly individuals. These diagnoses are in turn the subdivisory disorders of chronophilia, a more general term for any limitation of sexual love to individuals living within fixed age limits; chronophilia is in turn a paraphilia, a yet more general term familiarly of biomedical application that describes the misdirection of sexual love as a whole, be it into babies, or non-human objects, or images of suffering, or corpses. It will be obvious that the history of diagnostic refinement in pathologization is at least nominally a case of clinical hellenism; hellenism is itself a word adapted out of its original meaning, which was "the acknowledging and adoring of a multitude of Gods", to fit the less immoderately orgiastic definition "Graecism" in thought or speech. The criminal use of desire would be very grating in Kurdish.

But all sex is barbaric. We *are* the pleasures we enjoy, the blisses we admire; and all sex is a text, wingbats in a gaping slang. I adopt Hazlitt's position on the immortality ode because my mother was an alcoholic.

Freud said that my early biological hermaphrodism led to my original predisposition to bisexuality, which in the course of my development was reduced to monosexuality, leaving slight remnants of the stunted sex. The idea of development truly is formidably legitimate; and yet it is only the first of many ideas, each one more legitimate than the next. My infancy was an original predisposition to sexual love for children, which over the course of our development was reduced to sexual love for teenagers, and then, as if conclusively, to the same for adults; the elderly are terminally attractive but I would rather not suck them. Infant love is as durable as life. If it isn't, it must be. Immortality must mean the preterition of ageing, so that universal love may be comprehensive, that is, paedohebeëpheboteleiophiliac (omitting the elderly, who are ostentatiously not immortal); the sum of all disorders is the law of paradise. You can disagree with it but you can't disobey it. That's the bottom line.

1.2

There is a disconnect between the people and real politics. Meanwhile imaginary life, its dead end leavened unto the breach in its primitive control order, will insist on scavenging up the one aisle of definitively unshiftable goods, absolute for a bargain; the symptom of its being a currency is not to say the point of it. These odes are an only deficiently reorderable anagram whose letters don't all move laughed at during oral sex, a subtitle for everything we are. Trotsky said that the genetic links between the cow and the ameoba are immaterial for practical thinking, since the farmer is interested only in the *individual* qualities of the udder. Ringfence the spheres, universal benefits. Never middle yet too squeezed. The problem with perfectionism in poetry is the same as it is in sex: *all* ejaculation is premature. But perfectionism once abandoned will return to make you very stupid, as if you laugh in the wind summoned as a reprimand by your mother your face will not in truth stay like that. Roman watched me glide past in a dress. I returned to the bedroom and probably did something like another line. We thought that was completely hilarious, she did and I. She kissed me in the toilets for fifteen minutes and I did the same. I laughed at that. No-one in the queue will complain because everyone in the queue enjoys being impatient to do something illegal; the wait is nonetheless too long for being intrinsic. Our pretext is that when the doorman comes we will seem to be kissing, which meant really kiss; you said my mouth was softer than you expected after passion made you think I was constructed to be rough. The problem with conceptualism duplicates the one made earlier, pornography *replaces* sex and art; its originality is its provocation. Baudelaire and Gautier were nuns compared to us, transgeneric Cambridge hashishistas. You become radical when the only thing you can do to rouse the sleeping public is something truly catastrophic. Catastrophe is the thinking man's prosthesis. His belief is that in the face of grand projects to change the world, ordinary life is dispensable; on that basis the poet is his natural ally.

*

There is somewhere in infinite space a world that does not roll within the precincts of mercy, and as it is reasonable to suppose that there is music in heaven, in those dismal regions perhaps the reverse of it is found, made sweetly by the negroes unmasked by the author of 'An Arundel Tomb', for their private functions; those who neglect to please us are not doing it properly. But of which administration could less of what be said and never heard again for what? *Obama's?* The administration of modernism is to be difficult on purpose, to love the confusion of others as much as your own. Melody is exchanged for atonality, proving their trail by fungibility; however much these words dispirit me I love the experience of making them. These feet are made for dragging. There are propositions we do in all candour believe in but would never applaud, such as that the children of Tony Blair should be trepanned, or just grow up to be miserable schizophrenics, for suspicion that silence would be left empty, or our wrists slapped off, or of sounding like a fascist. But fear is neglected, time and time again, until nothing really scares you just as previously a leaf stung all over by puslike dots mimetic of a fucking lost scream did invariably on the walk up through the house rise like a bubble high in carbonated honey on the market to get some sex, your mother in the bath next door, slumped, that ass poem by Christian Prigent; I suddenly feel dizzy, it's like my throat is mostly hanging out; phenomenology is a subterfuge for manifesting that the commodity is not primordial; Try doing it on coke.

*

Proudly insinuating that he is his own virus, "J.C." decided for the *Times Literary Supplement* that if you come across an avant-garde woman who is prepared to meet you even halfway, "you catch yourself thinking you've got it." His true Penelope comes to pick him up from Ogygia. The food energy in the typical ejaculation is 2.9 kJ, 0.0035% of the average helping of moussaka. Do you speak barbaric, or just fucking howl it? I remember wanting to go to bed with myself, my bed in particular, so that I could do anything I wanted to do, all to myself, since I knew everything I would want doing to me and who would do what. I alone would come in both my mouths. I would get down on all four knees and stretch wide my asses to invite in my cocks. One cock, *mine*, would be *way too big* for me and *way too hard*; the other, also mine, is antithetic to magnitude. Harder than a thousand bass teeth. I would talk down to myself, spit in my mouth, force me, I would grip my tongue in my ass. But I would not run my fingers through my hair or look directly into my eyes and say I love you.

*

Even Burke believed that we have no right to make a market of our duties.

*

The system is broken. We need to fix the system.
We need to fix the system. The system is broken.

*

Aristotle joked that love of people who are elsewhere is liable to be "watery". We use it for washing up the Africans, who are unfortunately not able to be omnipresent.

Vietnamization to versification, the euphuistic body count
corona of mental arithmetic impossible to crack
the bath water intransigently black,
and back. What you find there is that everything has
been left as it was. The TV on, the oil on the fridge, the
records all over the floor; but under the window a
bridge is waiting, on the face of Deborah. Moronic acid
is a triterpenoid; traumatic acid heals by division. "This
grand magician whose art commands nature has
selected for his palace nothing but this obscure grotto."
One of your last texts said that you wanted to kiss my
soul. I fall in an infinite sheet of immaculate light.

1.3

It's the 1960s. You ask to see the manager, only to be
told, gradually, patiently, in innumerable stages, that
you are the manager, and then asked, all at once, would
you like the person who is complaining to be ejected,
since it is you? We who bite the other hand are
whatever is being itself.
It's impossible to bypass the first intoxications of
sadism forever, gambling on a new age old age; you
can ask the manager if you can find her why the exit is
so dismally far away.
Olson may be followed to the universe, but not to
Yucatan; what remains of us is systemicide, the frugal
blossoming of the void.
The void is final. Children are naturally quick to fidget,
making up for their denaturation by deficiency in peace
and incest: soppy inverted Schlemihls reinventing the
wheelspin on ice.
Or on sand, belabouring Iraq, withering like the Greek
marble industry,

Daughters of catastrophe, abandoned to the moon,
I'm only reality but digging in your forehead
where reason is not the irony for you but the opposite is
true, Leonie crawling from the tent with a new virginity
that moment inherited, to declare to my owner who laughs
in sympathy and knowledge at the innocence I bring
like a baby animal into the language of adults, that I opened
myself to show her what I was down there, because she asked
for that, and I couldn't yet care what it meant
to myself that I barely had yet, or even what it meant to her,
or whether I was truly thrilled right then and there,
only that by getting out the thing she asked to see
its secrecy became its truth, and what it did for me
became its end, mirroring the primary exchange
on credit of this impossible flame, hunger not eternity;
I dissipate superficiality forever until I explode there.

ODE TO TL61P 5

1.1

I stupidly broke the catch. I slammed the door shut and the catch encased in the door is now broken. The catch inside the rim is fine, and if I lodge a spoon in there it continues to function, but obviously then the door isn't closed. I am having a nightmare finding a replacement door. I have managed to take the door off. But I can't seem to get the door apart to remove the catch itself. A liquid sieve was slicked on mock extinct. The grating is a waste grown empty, ground up in the missing cogs; the ultimate multifacets grow facetiously immortal. For who knows well it isn't; she wants more than that, and so should you; please as if gradually read all the notes on your coding notice; it's good to know the worst, it's good to know that it's only that; Perturbation theory leads to an expression for the desired solution in terms of a formal power series in some small parameter that quantifies the deviation from the exactly solvable problem. Love can be trusted not to fade, as also faded out to trust; devour the wind that just washes over you, its meaning is its filling; your reflection in glass blown into the shape of your face to accommodate its progressive jutting; cracks appear in your shambolic argumentative scream learnt fresh from first orgasming, a rondo to oblivion *d'exécution transcendante*; excess levity leads to an unblessed strain injury for the dozen or so marketing executives secretly pretending to get good enough at free improvisation; they're out back; whatever the fuck that thought is, *get it back*; commissioning variations on your theme – the screen blinks, Yemen for cubist; get it back; mortality is scrambled to the précis of our meaning, to make life comprehensively succinct; the immutable is better than the mutable, the inviolable is better than the violable, and the incorruptible is better than the corruptible: look at teeth, or Africa. Or Wales. Look at yourself. You don't need to be Dante.

I go on to the mound. It is snowing a bit. The fence at the corner is obscurely associated with being loved and doing the creosoting for a meagre sum which I think is a lot but is also a way of rounding into the street with your feeling of disappointment. Twigs scratch and knock on it, later redone in local colour. People are dragging back the sled. On the top the snow is packed onto the muddy grass oddly hard by all their feet. That is the efficiency of feet. People go down the mound. In the summer when the snow was gone under the mud I went there with David and ended up agreeing to be the one who was fucked so long as I did not have to be the one who would fuck back, and put myself on my hands and knees with my pants down, in front of him, facing away; I felt myself become a hole, I now think I emerged as a hole for him; I now emerge as a hole for you. We didn't get to do it, our mothers came looking for us and stopped it even before fear did, but I suspected even then that he was frightened or just indifferently disgusted, since otherwise surely he would have done it to me quicker, since I think so; I mean that him fucking me would have come first, but not me fucking him, or our mothers; we should have made our mothers come too late; I heard that he told people about it and I was angry because I was ashamed at having again capitulated to secrecy; secrecy was my enemy, like God engrossed in someone else; in the caravan in his garden I tried pressing him to agree to one last fuck without touching with his father figure who was a man I now give a cartoon nose, white skin, a beard, and idly establish was 40. I'm colouring in his hair, it's brown. It wasn't love, but it hurt and left me complex; I am a real hole for you, not a barely noticeable flimsy crack; David had a stupid way of laughing and a fucking ugly blush. Hasten defections. I swapped stickers with him, and went on to exchange my motorbike for Christian's tank, an agreement which my father unhappily replied was a sort of extortion from infancy, but which made me sexually delight in having given away more than I had got back, for the delight was secret; I made my sister wear the fantasy lieutenant's shirt with the felt tip arrows pinned to the collar. To propitiate invasion. Nylon for Insignia. I lay under a cushion and asked her to jump on my head. She did. I like Roxette, *Elite* and cocoa butter on carrots.

10/11/10

The police smack the people in Merrion Row, doing their jobs justice; at Millbank the windows are booted down, voiding reinforcement; the government boys look set to make our solvency heroic; their genitals in plaster deck the halls like powerdrills;

You walk from the Strand to Nelson, left at the corner into Whitehall; the police are instructed to ingratiate camerapersons, by ignoring them; the technique is borrowed right from the top, tolerance of poverty is its paradigm; you film them and they film you, synergy by right;

Because the universe has been outmanoeuvred, individuals flourish; to put away your childish things, cut the arts first; say in the prophylactic tone of establishment sarcasm; what chance for debt reduction against the sheer nobility of sentiment;

If there will be a revolution in the UK, it will require the army; war will continue either way, sugared by truth or not; love is not the unswerving professional bias of police dogs; it has to be made from scratch at the first indication of its possibility.

The French have their *avantages à qui*, as we in turn have ours; a peine rentrés les lampions, voilà que tombent les bonnes; if we don't fight now, the super-rich will harden into sultans; deeply and truly fuck them, one-way receptacles;

At the corner of Parliament Square the teenagers are standing on bus shelters; they are shouting for what they believe and feeling what you never will; think of the anger you waste on gifts that might be used on money; masturbation is not love, it's betrayal of the workers;

You can see the predisposition to moderate success in politics; in the features of Aaron Porter, the flexible physiognomy; the thought of sex with him doesn't occur to the majority of his delegates; that's what makes him perfect for redefining compromise;

The wall of glass smashed in, looks like what Wordsworth saw; in the flint windbreaker, lying on the empty floor; to be a shard of broken glass, shining like life; psychosis as the mirror of your dreams, or justice;

A cop with a freshly bandaged face is the punctum of the coverage; her wide eyes make fear emblematic, glint on film intensely; at Sussex they grabbed them and chucked them down the slope to be arrested; at the bottom of the slope the women on minimum wage count the minutes of grind;

I'm far from knowing what to do about any of

this, or after it; but so long as my blood is attached to the world I live for by its motion; I create this pledge in utter solemnity, I will never deny it; but burst to make its love for everyone shower from my heart.

The west Irish had nothing but tiny scraps of land with a cabin, a pig and potatoes; but Belfast and Dublin had England. Love gets saner, stained into the glass. All countries must work together toward a mutual resolution of currency imbalances, or risk war, says the governor of the Bank of England, tasked with making the genital stage of Godzilla inevitable; but he is right, it's the answer Jesus would give if pressed; the severance will yet amount to minus sweet fuck all. Your job is to be at that orgy and to experience maximum anxiety, write, and see what happens; it's not a joke to say that you learn from that, except you decline. Synergized to social fact, surplus grout of the myriad equivalents; at the source I is screaming or am; the consummated Islamabad dispatches rolled into a prolegomenon to an epigram. Smoke that shit. *Yes*. Passion swings both ways, unfixed to be enlarged, hungry for the majority of the earth. Robert's penis is a surprise. In my tent, it is more pink than I am. I am more red or purple or brown. I had guessed, startling me, but I sucked it anyway, not to go back; I think it was an excruciation to him and a probably morally significant embarrassment, because he never used it against me when I started punching his face in on the couch at my mother pissed herself on; get it back; why did I do that, smacking around with childish fists, deepening our wishes, blunting life in him and me; or smack that miniscule nameless boy who merely explained to me that my fantasy car for sale to him could be given wheels, when I wanted it to be flat and just glide? The Victorian English had their more innocent Green Zones in India, from which to perorate on the superiority of peace for trade; indiscreet to go slaughtering around all over the place like the Russians via the French and in any case very likely more overheads to redemption. If sex is the price for that, be it what you may; after all sex disappears anyway.

Remembering nothing at all the right moments is difficult; so much of the rest of your time is exchanged for the lot; since poverty porn is the price of its spiritual opposite; what you get up to you pay for, come later; strikes are impossible unless you are quorate, don't be a speck and froth through the roof; Proudhon concealed that inflation is theft by being too famous about property; you are keeping it real; according to the definition of truth 'adequatio rei et intellectus', harmony depends on you being no better than a load of fucking things; there is no end to it; only at the end is the absolute ever what it is in truth; get what back; meanwhile regular people get impatient, adopt silence as compensation for their virtue in waiting for it; which I cannot do, and so am angry to think about; though I am not obliged to think about it; and I am not obliged to be angry either. 2. Compassion should be balanced and sustainable, like growth, not more balanced and more sustainable. Public sector workers will not solve your problem because they are net tax consumers, what you need is for people without any exposure to universalism to create the wealth. Wealth tastes better like that, anyhow. Less like Asian fusion. 3. The dream is finally to have no need of money of our own, like the government, but there is nothing to finalise; if you can't stymie their manipulations, you can settle for monitoring their surplus, but either way they're all the same, they leave you in the end for a *stärker Dasein*; a huge rope of blood the width of a golf bag falls out of his eye when you shoot into him, you are an heroic soldier; the kindness I have enjoyed has been more unusually beautiful from Hindoos than from Christians, and weirder; the very idea of a virgin birth is a slander against my sex; and yours too, whatever that is, whoever you are beside me; our tribute to the world is our desire, nothing else.

China is now a multilateral partner. That joke about the reference to the answer in the riddle in the reference to the answer to my life will be repeated without a pause until I laugh. Bush says *three* people were waterboarded, and hold the zeroes; our text today is *maintain physical integrity*, but a hundred times funnier, and therefore a hundred and one times funnier, billions of times funnier, and hereafter infinitely more funny because stupefying at a compound growth rate too big to fail. There is something we need to do about everything, something it is always hard to be. Career poets are part of the problem, smearing up the polish, drying out the fire; chucking shit all over the place; not being party to the solution; banking on the nodding head 'the reader' saying 'yes, that's what it's like' so as not to know what it's for, since meaning is easier that way, gaped at through the defrosted back window of the Audi, hence the spring for a neck; we all know where that shit got us: *being what we eat*. The British have become snobs. They don't *want* to be security guards always getting the night shifts at KFC illegally married to sewage technicians, subject to racist abuse which intelligent politicians learn they must not be seen on camera to regard as bigotry; the immigrants are real because they do. They say, I am more realistic than

you. But at least you listen. The EU ones are the
mainstream, the non-EU ones the avant-garde.

The real cause of massive growth in the size of the state
was fighting major wars: the majority public sector is
the wages of justice for crushing the fascists.

        Kissing softly round the true
        hole cut out of sanity
        the eyes I crossed out in a fantasy
        shine right through;
        to burn out the profounder hole
        resolved to being dead
        to love complaining in your head
        in your soul;
        our meaning is not an indulgence
        or capital all our blood
        distorting like a seed to bud
        in vengeance;
        our representatives will crush
        their lungs up like a piston,
        the Cheese Lenin grates his fist on
        your toothbrush,
        which I take for a sex toy, friction
        conceptually bleeds
        into agony, the fire feeds
        its fiction;
        the faces are all safely tucked
        in balls of knotted dream,
        make the mystery face scream
        or get fucked;
        what in either case they sing
        only as they go
        back to block up the thing you go
        mad needing.

Reconciliation with your mother on top of Spinozistic
macroeconomics. What's
the intractable thing you did? Splitting to the eye,
whose camera will zoom in, you're meant to
brood, Fuck wish-fulfilment.
The light of truth to life back at wavering
blackout bypass. Possibility
is apocryphal impossibility. Neither is the best,
Take what's coming to you. Massification
is light. We writhe on the bed in a slalom of air
Obstinate star, I don't really want to stop moving, we are
different.
Creationism is
a tedious joke about the superiority of love to maths. In
compensation
I don't know what I am for all my only life, so what
When you first start waiting the vertical limit is
everything left to define. But it fills up, mouth the galaxy;
beauty scratches your tongue out. Floating
behind the disguise is a chewed-off thread of elastic. Impersonated
love absconds to scapegoat paradise. *f*
Smile out a window. Shimmering under tenderness, sex
and rage; the vertical limit is past the unlimited
average, in the everything aisle;
pornography is *like that*, it's not going to bite you,
you're the wrong flavour, you taste used. Learn to
barely smile at it, induce your dispersal in objects. The
value of objects begins in you, is human originality;
humanity consists in making everything unsustainable
by definition. The objects this this this and this or this
this this and this: Racine, air, blackmail of irides, a
spat sun shot of testosterone; the open fridge, stars,

seduction, old cool moons of saliva; Norman Lamont's
– pick anything – femur, Visa, pewter, ANC Regional
Chairperson Dickson Masemola; not your average
mind-bleed, nothing but the slops. Run away into the
pallid indefinite darkness, who burn up in it; the limit
of radiance is secrecy. But it is no secret that Anglo-Irish
wanted to pay out 40 million euros in bonuses, or that
it is possible to be either savage or civil about it.
The strategic advantage of the charmingly modernist
inferno of chic modernist rubbish, well presented
modernist rock and cracked, west-facing modernist
mud benefiting from a vespertinal crepusculum perfect
for masculine lamentation preferred to female hysteria
is that it can be reconstituted, practically at the flick of
a switch, by water, e.g. not otherwise than effortlessly.
This red rock and the budget chicken breast go word
for word. The sell-by date makes both poisonous, but
both are good for the margins. The whites of eyes of
whites whose rights are welts shine out their cries for
help.

Without cease I flatter and caress myself in the
prejudice that an infinite muteness will hide my
weakness. But my heart is too much oppressed and will
rend a discourse from me. I will speak to you this once,
then be silent forever. Ask not on what basis of hope
this fatal love that grips me is founded. I do not accuse
what pangs I hallucinate in Achilles who stoops to
dignify my suffering. The sky directs inhuman joy to
scramble at me every single trait of its hatred. Do I not
replay in terror that scene when you and I were tossed
into irons? I endured cruel hands that ravished me
without light or life for days. In the end my cheerless
eyes sought clarity, and I saw I was pressed in an arm
spattered with blood. I trembled, Doris, and was afraid

to be met with the face of a savage conqueror. I entered
his ship while detesting his fury, averting my gaze with
horror. Then I saw him. His face it turned out was not
horrible. I felt the reproach expire in my mouth. My
heart defined itself as my enemy, I forgot my ill
humour, I could do nothing but cry. I let myself be led
by that elect oleaginous Führer. I loved him at Lesbos,
I love him at Aulide. Iphigenia offers to protect me, but
in vain, extension of her hand is doomed to fail.
Miserable consequences of these furies by which I am
tormented. I only take

> the hand that she will give to me
>   to steel myself against her, who
> without revealing what I am
>   may live by her happiness, 1.3
> which I cannot myself suffer.

*

These are the hardest passages to write through, when
there is nothing on the other side but the exhaustion of
the claim to be there. Was I more beautiful as a child
than I am now? Will the sexual relationship between us
be forever unequal, me wanting him more than he
wants me? That child with the very probably more
honourable claim to beauty, is he also my fucking
father? Fucking my mother before I fucking existed?
Do I *want* myself in the hope that I want something
beautiful, at all? If I don't is that freedom from what
you fucking want? Do I too easily forget how much I
used to want myself in the future, how gorgeous I was
to me when I was imaginary? How sexy I was in my
dreams before I existed. How much more fucked I was
before I fucked. How much more fuckable right then if
not yet strictly fuckable. Yet really how easy to fuck.

But fuck how fucking fuckable I was before I fucking
fucked up fucking by becoming fucking fucked. How
hard the thought of barely having started living made
me. I did desire myself then, but *not* as someone who
is less of anything, e.g. older, not invariably; I wanted
myself with identical eyes and an asshole blissed out
on the Spring. Why is God into virgins? But now I
look back, that boy doesn't arouse me very much in
truth. I'd sooner drown in bed forever with the women
from my twenties, painting a sky of orgasms, acting
insoluble. I remember the number I had beautiful sex
with but not their total number. Or mine. Trotsky on
the publication by the Bolsheviks of the secret treaties
between the Tsar and his western allies, 22nd November
1917: "Secret diplomacy is a necessary tool for a propertied
minority which is compelled to deceive the majority in
order to subject it to its interests. Imperialism, with
its dark plans of conquest and its robber alliances and
deals, developed the system of secret diplomacy to the
highest level. The struggle against the imperialism which
is exhausting and destroying the peoples of Europe is at
the same time a struggle against capitalist diplomacy,
which has cause enough to fear the light of day. The
Russian people, and the peoples of Europe and the
whole world, should learn the documentary truth
about the plans forged in secret by the financiers
and industrialists together with their parliamentary and
diplomatic agents. The peoples of Europe have paid
for the right to this truth with countless sacrifices and
universal economic desolation." In the overture to
absolute knowledge we are all the phantasmagoric
sexual molestation charge "from Sweden"; ordinary
children grow up into the bankocracy the better to
remain speculative in private. Nothing left behind. Sound
familiar. *L'Art d'Ali Bongo.* Human loot.

You become in secret my original accumulation of what you are forever lost for. *Mine* gets hard in my mouth, I will die if I cut it out. You are *mine*, and become in the open my prodigal frittering of what you are left. What I am is narrow left, gems to glue and shun in iron, to flurry on the air now breathed on very far away; but not your genitals or eyes both shining in the same way from joy as you shut and shape me to infinity O love I am forever not yet dying This is my secret, I am the reason that is always left to say, the torment which is its necessity. *Mine* means that impossible clinging on. Men of Athens, in all things fiscal you shall henceforth be too superstitious. What you are now is not lost but forever reshelved. *The Workers*: Boo. Who said what? See now that I, I am He, the memories that run / ahead pronounce the prospect dead, you see that now. Behind whose cyst a sycophantic skeleton shoves love up an inarticulate cretin; count me up and down, gently too rapid; the dark is on secondment in our flesh, burning at the limit of our light. The object revolves in the way on the road the elastic snaps to drop the subject, bouncing to the central reservation is a scream. You hear it.

Di

Hearing

nk in.

Since the frame is loose it buzzes,
which is so grating on the ear

stitched up on rebooted muses
auscultated away in fear.

There is no room alive inside
my life for shit or milk to fill
but what you sabotage or hide
in dreams replied the window sill.

However that may be bullshit
not being maternal is free
flowing away to our credit
jurisdiction of secrecy.

As in reality you trust
the flee clause *paradis fiscal*
inserts to make the children lust
infinitely to age et al.

But the US treasury blocks
the Libyan thirty billion
liberating the flesh from shocks
to profit in palliation.

So that there are both stops and starts
computed again and again
in homage to the sister arts
of universal love and pain.

Marx said the Greeks were normal children, not that
you can eat their fingers or love everything in the
wrong way or patently rip off their infinity. Your
infinity is the irreversible backlash. Burnt milk can't be
sucked too hard, cold milk won't go down; but the rest
that will be forever, the final cut, ultimate budget,
deceptively simple twists on the similes of eschatology,

checkouts etc, the last page of Aeschylus, Aslan's cum, TL61P, a giant asshole with fire extinguishers for teeth, I fly from fads in attitude to my eternal gratitude, *träges Kartoffelblut*, human to the end, you are a dead end, the Danny Boy incident.

Bid for dreams by stretching is natural, cleaning your teeth is moral, too; blinded by the bright idea you had to see your living through; in battered cod, the probing tongue is flattered at the oiled bone; what effort to survive beyond the filleting for me; it's the same with Palestinian corpses on BBC News. Don't worry too much if you don't get absolutely all the off the when you first start. The idea at the beginning is to get *some*. You started it. Increasing as the screenings multiply, what's your fucking problem in the future? That we do not know yet. The phantoms will be harnessed, made to slam the freezer door, which expertly connected to a dynamo concealed inside the fridge below will cause to rupture in a glow the infinite equivalent energy of a world unborn measured in the potential of future Siberian oil, justifying the Japanese; II Bidding for dreams is *this* natural your teeth is moral, too: think errors in scanning; under the *that* head of the pillow of labour is bloody, bright idea: squint at the National Drug Code sequestered in the UPC; nations of the mind retail the higher purposes of purchase *this*: zero-compressed symbology; ash in cod, necrotic everything *that* isn't on fire, but rips: the imperial addition of the EAN; thrown off for the screen *this* the meaning multiplies into the dreamy dark: exchanged via a GS1 eCom message; in the *that* future we do not know the ghost is made to swing at all: but a mere GS1 EPC tag for Global Individual Asset Identifier; *this* the freezer door, which expertly connected to a dynamo: life on

Yoopsie; concealed inside the fridge below *that* will cause the infinite: licking Laurer's rigid guard bar; the energy *this* of a thousand suns, measured in spitting milk: Polaris strung out over Troy, Ohio.

III

Bidding for natural errors under the UPC nations of the mind higher purchase zero-compressed ash in cod isn't on fire but rips the EAN for the screen in the dark exchanged GS1 eCom message; in the future we know is made to swing a GS1 EPC tag for Global Individual Asset Identifier; this is the freezer door obviously expertly concealed below the infinite Laurer's sheer drop.

JENKINS, MOORE AND BIRD
2015

Jenkins, Moore and Bird

Eine Revolution ist ein reines Naturphänomen

Exchangeable for the wave equivalent to its crack in the shadow grows less and more psychic. What action alone can never imagine of reality awash with rival surf. A slider body single-crystal diamond low the shadow surface later overlooking Malibu Beach at high velocity. Not without regret this scene is screwed into the wall with a spinning drill. There is surplus reality for the body leading trailing edges to its top and sides a pair of spaced-apart realities in parallel air attached to the sides and downward from the real surface air-bearing each together surface and the slider body also section distance from the trailing edge toward the leading edge. This is where the asset can be static and its slow exchange for a latitudinally equivalent crack grows psychic. For only where a single-crystal diamond attached to the slider body in reality is ringfenced in the section where together only diamond bottom surface is substantially coplanar with the air now held together at an edge that causes cracking is the asset at velocity the head. Every day this sudden shower of coins escaping Malibu is craved. For when the head flies very near the surface is increased the chance it may crash into large asperities. To a head that crashes it is too late to be stopped into the asset where however its existing makes it hard to be.

•

Exchangeable for its proscription the wave already equivalent to its cut or crack in the shadow disk asperities grows less alone more edgy and go-to proto-psychic. What this act alone does can now never be imagined in the hills of a rectangular reality awash with rival surf.

There a slider body having a single-crystal diamond flies in low above the shadow surface overlooking Malibu Beach as for the disk it altogether now uncolours is rotated at a high angular velocity. Not without regret or surplus this scene too is screwed into the cold wall with a colder spinning drill. Where there is reality for the body having leading and trailing edges to its top and bottom surfaces and sides having a pair of spaced-apart subrealities in elongated substantially parallel air-bearing members being attached to the sides and extending downward from the real bottom surface alone the air-bearing members each together having an air-bearing surface and the slider body also having a removed section of post-reality extending for a distance from the trailing edge toward the leading edge. This is where the asset can be hedged in static not escaping where its slow exchange for the erasure of the soul already equivalent to its crack grows proto-psychic. For only where a single-crystal diamond fixedly attached to the slider body whose reality alone is ringfenced in the projected removed section where together the single-crystal diamond having a bottom surface now alone substantially coplanar with the air-bearing surfaces held together at an edge that causes cracking of asperities the asset is located on the media as the media rotates at high velocity relative to the head. Every day this shower of coins escaping from Malibu airspace is craved so that at the flying height alone of the disk it is reduced so that asperities on the surface of the media may be absolutely clear to interact without the head. For example when a head flies very near the surface there is now an increased chance it may actually crash into large asperities projecting together up from its shadow surface over on the disk. To avoid a head that crashes reality it is desirable too late that simply the disk escape the asperity-free surface which alone is predictable for its eternity of starting and stopping on promotion in the asset where however unfortunately existing manufacturing processes make it sadly difficult to achieve an asperity-free shadow together.

•

Morning the size of a kidney. Peg dolls, chewed, equivalent, crushed.

•

Every limb of wasted life is in a parallel universe that it is too late to sequence in darkness matched to identical reaching in. The uvula too before it spreads will isolate in wasted life the failure hard to imagine in the untranslated severance. Leave the acid in these regions that mean that the dream is a reality. Responsible disposal of the wasted oesophagus ascending in these does not presume invasion more than dream. The sequences of the region wasted and the wasting sequence block. Flanking human regions with their corresponding sequences in the exemplary psychotic rat and wasted chicken. Condone the apparition of a bucket. Spitting corn oil any dream. Reason as waste of reality in breadcrumbs where there is only the sentiment of the mechanism. Expression of that wasted sentiment and its evolutionary origin of waste and abnormal expression laid bare. Analysis of structures and isolation for days of cardiac actin. Aorta-type human model for vertebrate ultimately a waste exploited out of restriction. Just within reach you edge to the drop. Shelter yet becomes a storm whose shadow you are wasted to isolate.

•

Every limb of Roger Bird or subdivision thereof is in principle a human DNA library. Every chromosome wasted on his tonsils in ongoingness contains an entire wasted parallel universe of amino acid sequences. It is futile or too late to deduce today these sequences in darkness from the waist up nucleotide matched to identical sequences from the β-actin. Only reaching in to nip the uvula before it spreads waste to Doncaster will isolate the wasted recombinant phage carrying the cytoplasmic β-actin gene. The consequences of a failure to act in time are hard to imagine in the untranslated region who knows how many nucleotides upstream from the ATG initiation codon. But severance of the uvula of waste alone still leaves the tear ducts, not to mention the penis of pure waste. The homology of acid sequences in these regions does not mean that the dream of nasolacrimal micturition is ultimately a reality. Roger Bird cannot piss out of his eyeballs. But grouting of the tear ducts and responsible disposal of the penis of pure waste alone still leaves the wasted oesophagus, not to mention the sober inescapable ascending colon. Homology in these does not presume the pragmatic upward removal of nutrients through billions of mobile bacteria assisted by a detectable tilt of the epiglottis to prevent laryngeal invasion by waste is more than a dream. Roger Bird cannot shit up his own gullet. The DNA sequences of the coding region, the untranslated region and the sequence block of waste between the "CCAAT" box and "TATA" box in the flanking DNA of the human β-actin gene are highly homologous with the corresponding sequences of the psychotic rat and wasted chicken β-actin genes. But while the homology of sequences in these regions with their corresponding sequences in the exemplary rat and chicken both wasted and psychotic does condone the apparition of a bucket of deep-fried medieval plague, the same cannot be said of Roger Bird, who is not to date fumigated in spitting corn oil in any dream that stands to reason wasted on the pettiest reality in pestilential breadcrumbs, where there is no point but only the sentiment of a point. The regulatory mechanisms of wasteful expression of the sentiment and its wasted evolutionary origin and probable involvement in wasting abnormal expression and diseases are laid bare in the analysis of its structures and organization. The isolation for 7 days of the Roger Bird wasted human cardiac muscle actin gene and Roger Bird wasted human aorta-type smooth muscle actin gene and Roger Bird wasted human stomach-type smooth muscle actin gene proposes a model for wasting vertebrate actin evolution. Ultimately our homology is exploited out of restriction endonucleases purchased from Bethesda Research Laboratories. But feel deep into that scramble of born and dead where use as a wasted whole includes without the least regulatory prejudice ecstatic use cracked out of the synthetic inequality index. Old bondage whose waste of new shadow you isolate in a shelter that becomes the storm it breaks.

•

Early morning, tacked to the body. Peg dolls, erasure, bucket, isolate.

•

The face of things is open and familiar to what toxic blood escaping in submissive vapours warping export concrete pump trucks towed down to the late abyss in storage one by one trembling into functionality, including a viewer optional free improved alignment quantity useless to calculate broken links to the structural open one by one. Each bends to each other shouting *parler de ma flamme* the lives get out. As one by one each dreams converted into dreaming braces for a broken dream neck unconverted dream break into song. I am set in Richmond, Virginia. This place represents to me the end of the line and the origin strewn in its middle beyond one place that is the definition of what is life out of reach. I am within reach and at present disappointed to be put in a flat that crushes me with my carpet covered in huge stains I cannot get out that I made already before I got in. The stains are surveyed until they are pressed into a dotplot graph viewer. The person I fake there is here to blame. It speaks to you about my flame. It is a superpower as will appear. For here represents the end of the line and the origin in its own middle that is so far beyond it there is no point is a representation too: look at that foot on the bed that never existed that we got when that never existed. Since then everything has been for that.

•

The face of things is open and familiar to all. But it has to be primed in toxic blood to shut. Strange, submissive vapours, sunlight warping export concrete pump trucks, towed down to the brink of the late abyss in storage where, one by one, in trembling we come into our functionality, including a dotplot graph viewer as standard, optional modelling tools, one free improved 3D alignment viewer and a quantity it is useless to escape calculating of broken links to the database of structural similarities, carved wide open one by one to give at random Moore and Bird. Each bends to the other shouting *que je revienne encor vous parler de ma flamme* as one by one and all by none the lives we get go out. As one by one dreams preserved to sustain them are converted into braces of coconut oil lost on the radiator for dream necks that the unconverted dream one by one breaks into song go out. I am in Richmond, Virginia. Here this place represents to me the end of the line and the origin positioned in its middle beyond it that are one place that is the definition of what is life out of reach. I am there and within reach on a temporary contract, and I am disappointed to be found set in a flat that crushes me with its own carpet covered in huge stains I cannot get out that I must have made already before I got in. The stains are surveyed one by one until they are exactly indiscriminate pressed into a dotplot graph viewer of grey grown indiscriminate. The waking person that I fake is there and blaming capital which is in fact to blame. When I come it is to speak to you my flame. It is a superpower as will appear. That being here represents to me the end of the line and the origin in its own middle that is so far beyond it there is no point dying is a representation too: look at that foot on the bed that never existed. The life we got to when that foot on the bed did exist never existed. Do not get to exist because since then everything is the same. The face of things is open to that too.

•

The upstairs neighbour won't stop fucking. Good for him but all the worse for us. The wind is not from far enough outside but only just. Trauma is everywhere and also not everywhere, only in you but also not only in you, in fact always in you but also in fact never in you. Imagine a world where that would be true and where the senses are revived to their native mortality. Nothing that is everywhere but is also not everywhere or only in you but is also not only in you or always in fact in you but is not also never in fact in you. How does it feel to divide up Malibu Beach, you antithesis of my single fire, slated for the stateless fantasia? What about continuing to grow up right now while keeping childhood too? I get the way that pain can be forsaken, by exceeding the injury it proves. There can be no better demonstration of the plausibility of destiny for so long as love alone is destiny.

•

Whoever prevents us from giving our best is among its predestined victims. With effort the tongue can be slipped right through his mouth into the endocranial cavity and the core of nightmare: time. We mistake this destination if we can stop at it once it is entirely fucked up at last. The destination already can never be stopped at when you are there. You are not going to pretend it is there because instead you pretend it never existed.

•

Lord Green who as a matter of principle will not comment on business past or present is waiting for an answer in the pig-sty. Rate him in intellecticons. Watch the assets pile up in hipster plankton gore. The world deserves the best we have to give because the best we have to give is what will fuck up capital most. Why do people not want to give up the best they have to give unless they have to and are put to it. Lord Green prevents us from giving our best and is among its predestined victims. With a little effort the tongue can be slipped right up through the roof of his mouth, through the septum and into the endocranial cavity and the core of nightmare: time. We mistake even this predestination if we think we can stop at it once capital is entirely fucked up at last. Even this predestination already cannot be stopped at later: you are there. But just as you are there it now is gone. Because you are not going to pretend it is there just because you are, instead you pretend it never existed.

•

Morning size of a kidney. Peg dolls, blaming, equivalent, crushed.

•

I have tried to make us communicate, but it is hard for me, sending you the same thing, communication, a rectangle of mackerel, over and over again, delighted when you are bored of pretending it has a meaning, ecstatic when you have had enough of getting it, thrilled when you allow yourself to be faintly exasperated to have allowed the point where you are ready to expect anything you are sent to be intimate to vanish or fade, or to stretch still to a relevant dream of intimacy, repeated in the cupboard under the stairs among vibrating restraints in the garage with the loud-opening door you open by tugging a vertical cord that now excitingly is shut, where in this noise and silence we set out for here again.

•

Yes, the Realities of Life, yes, bonded to terms like these. There is a dream in which you are escaping from guards who are running after you, on the orders of a Communist tyrant who in the scene is observed through its doorframe ragefully dictating incommunicable acts of retribution in guttural livid shorthand to be visited in the event of reality on the missing life now hatefully obscured and subcontracted to the deserving middle, screaming at inferiors at will aboard his massive passive tugboat of split-level grille, none of which need mean for now or any equal time like that when sense is lacked to work to stay alive, and guards are all-consumingly at large, where to evade arrest you squeeze your whole body under a mattress that in the dream is horizontal for on top of which there reappears a misplaced British military observer on standby to escape being sucked hollow, presumed innocent, actually in a pact with reality, now and forever, who to be absolutely clear is fucking the other soldier who is there, and once you are completely squeezed in under the mattress it is being done by that expert to her on, to excuse the imposition of a life directly under his peacekeeping pounding ass, you explain without meaning it or strangely caring that who should be free and at large on the tugboat must risk being apprehended, in retro grammar sparely aped like that, to your profit, since he, the observer now rationalised with then beseeched, whatever prop he also is, why ever he is there, whatever only option you can take, makes a show of being persuaded by these words enough to let you go under, since for that moment by an eligible minimum of exact resemblance you are his comrade in the navy, loose on the destroyer of desire, and might yet get to be his total comrade by a quantity of exact resemblance approximating even the authentic, but for your knowledge of its de-escalating effects, so as while being essentially non-stick all over, still somehow actually to bear, since there is no other option, stuffing your whole body under the mattress and curling up there, despite his manifestly not being about to discontinue his fuck on it, love held up at breaking point where one more push will end it all, come, all ye faithful, and once inescapably you are there, tucked in discreetly as the predicament merits between the base grid of black metal springs and the overhead white rectangle you keep dead still. And for what is a reason you think should exist but are ready to know by yourself, even the whole evasively *your, stuffed-in* body doesn't upset the mattress it is alive under or function to make it combust or disastrously tilt, or represent an unmanageable unsexy lump or protuberance pressed down in militant unison with gravity that would thwart any wound-up military man in the execution of a proper clockwork fuck, not in this dream, despite being exactly then as now exactly its actual size and shape. After puberty you simply don't grow any more. Under the mattress you lay your arms out crosswise on your chest. In the ear pressed down against black metal springs are later heard and condescendingly listened to some mortal intimations of a tinnitus for eels: we are slaves too and we live with it, the alternative is madness and starvation. The guards do come, twice, eventually first then right away, and when they do come are observed at once, looking for you. But for striations of that moment gambled on a flat percentage of its untold parallels in infinity's unpaid overtime, cut to the square of zero hours, you suddenly are transformed into, or simply now suddenly get at last to be, Roger Moore, not only someone you are not but, worse, a walking wasted opportunity to find a proper object with a bit of contemporary traction. Instead you end up not even the epitome of anything. As the mattress bulges, identity wavers back to him. Negatives drop from heaven bound in a shower of seminal sleet. You are not some other actor you once could have been, or had once wanted to be, or were once told you ought to be, or once could list, or later had it known to you without your ever really being spoken to that you will need to be, or couldn't find a way up to, or just naively went on thinking that you would obviously be at some point, or only once in your life never cared if you would ever be or not, but were not in any case, but him, Roger fucking Moore, as he might identify himself in anger to an erstwhile fan who had forgotten his name, by now scarcely an even vanishingly salient figure, worse than it sounds. So completely that before you know it you were born on 14 October 1927 in Stockwell, now part of the London Borough of Lambeth, the only child of a cis-policeman and his archaic housewife. You attended Battersea Grammar School and were evacuated to Holsworthy, Devon, during the war. You later attended the College of the Venerable Bede, but never graduated. The fit is almost wastefully exact, or else you split in two and say Untrue. What did the end of that story do at first but never stop again. Under conscious pressure, liberalised to the cognitive equivalent of light-touch community policing, your name is spectacularly descrambled into *groom, ogre, fuck more, germ, erogenous gore, me or who, her room, germoline,* and *ore* and is the substitute for the more primary Sean Connery, himself also more or less absolutely the utmost figure to pick. And I really do want to fuck more hard, just as the dream dictates, when you wake, each elastic thrust to bury love in no tomorrow. As Roger Moore for pretty much the duration under the mattress you are just slick and oily instead of in any way primarily hard, more fluent in civilian from your pidgin to your oratory, not prepared just to sit back and scream yourself sick, admittedly no longer compelling in the monotony of your plastic oversophistication, but indirectly mandatory as the best sublimated bright sadistic instinct, sexy to the wrong people, like the actual NSA. The guards cannot find you to apprehend now so they leave. At last the scene breaks out in scenery. We lay down together at the top of the hill in the thousands of wavering flowers, made level with all of the sky that extended so far that the fading and muting of distance on colour could openly paralyse and shine, and on the ground I held you and in you held me together. I love you is an easy thing to say, now you say it. Bind this life around our life insanely quick and tight: flood our perfect darkness with its own defected light. Since my earliest idea of you I have been shaking. Now I want you so much my skin is incessant wild electric. Identity is a death tax: fuck the dark away, become right. Down in the square where none of the whole dream can matter, not being caught signifies nothing less than whatever. Because you want to be caught. Secretly you want to be caught, to be made public, to be sexually reborn, to be extracted by love and purified, and made disgusting again. But here and now escaping on the non-stick agnostic Communist tugboat of articulated split-level grille and gore itself, this world where this would have to actually be done, on whose only top deck the anonymous Asiatic tyrant is bloodthirstily beheld in a blur of rubberstamping the warrant

for our arrest in an indelible sea of best-forgotten fathomless 57%
Mexican sexual froth, never being caught remains the indispensable
alibi for loving the wrong person forever.

•

For only where a single-crystal diamond attached to the slider body in
reality is ringfenced in the section where together and coplanar with
the air together at an edge alone that cracking is the asset in velocity
the head which in this dream is horizontal one by one the lives go
out can represent to me the end of every origin rotated to its middle
beyond one place that is life out of reach, where reality is the only
mechanism put simply of wasted evolutionary abnormal expression,
to wait there as the walls close in and out, set where what is true and
where the sense revived to native mortal fire and air, rips out the
cord now vertical from Doncaster to Richmond, waltzing Jenkins,
Moore and Bird to Bethesda Research Laboratories.